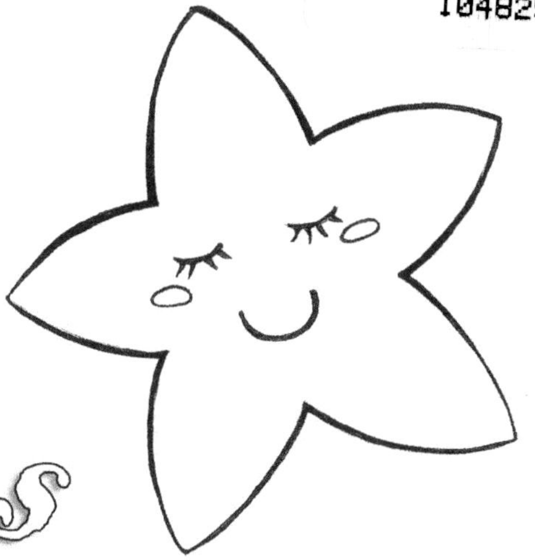

Cuties Attack

A book designed for coloring

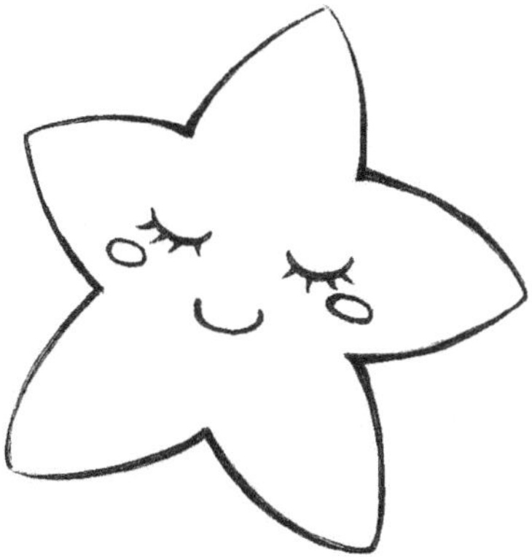

Queenie Wong

ISBN-13: 978-1532943614
ISBN-10: 153294361X
First published in United States in 2016
Illustrations by Queenie Wong
Wonger0050@yahoo.com.hk

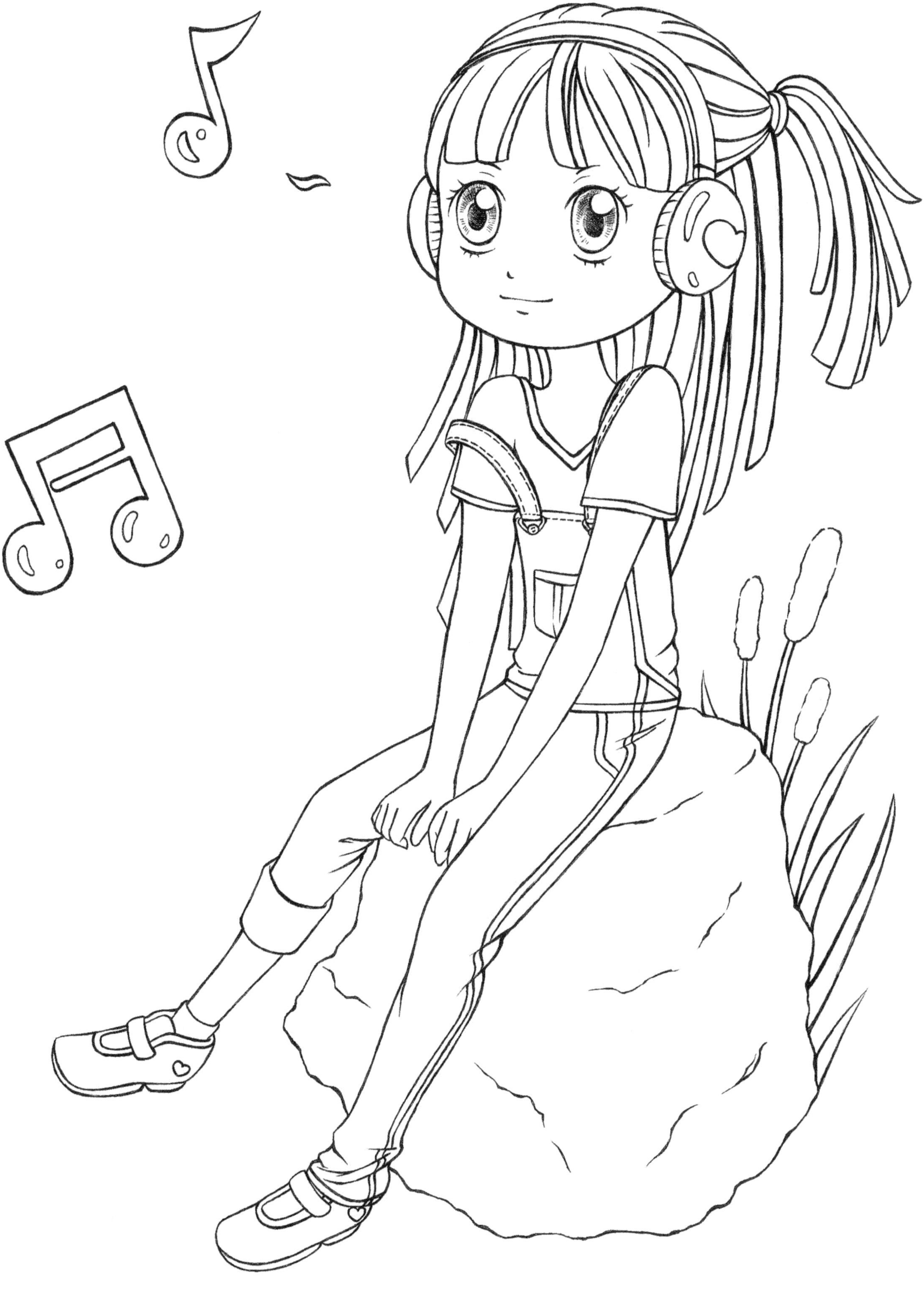

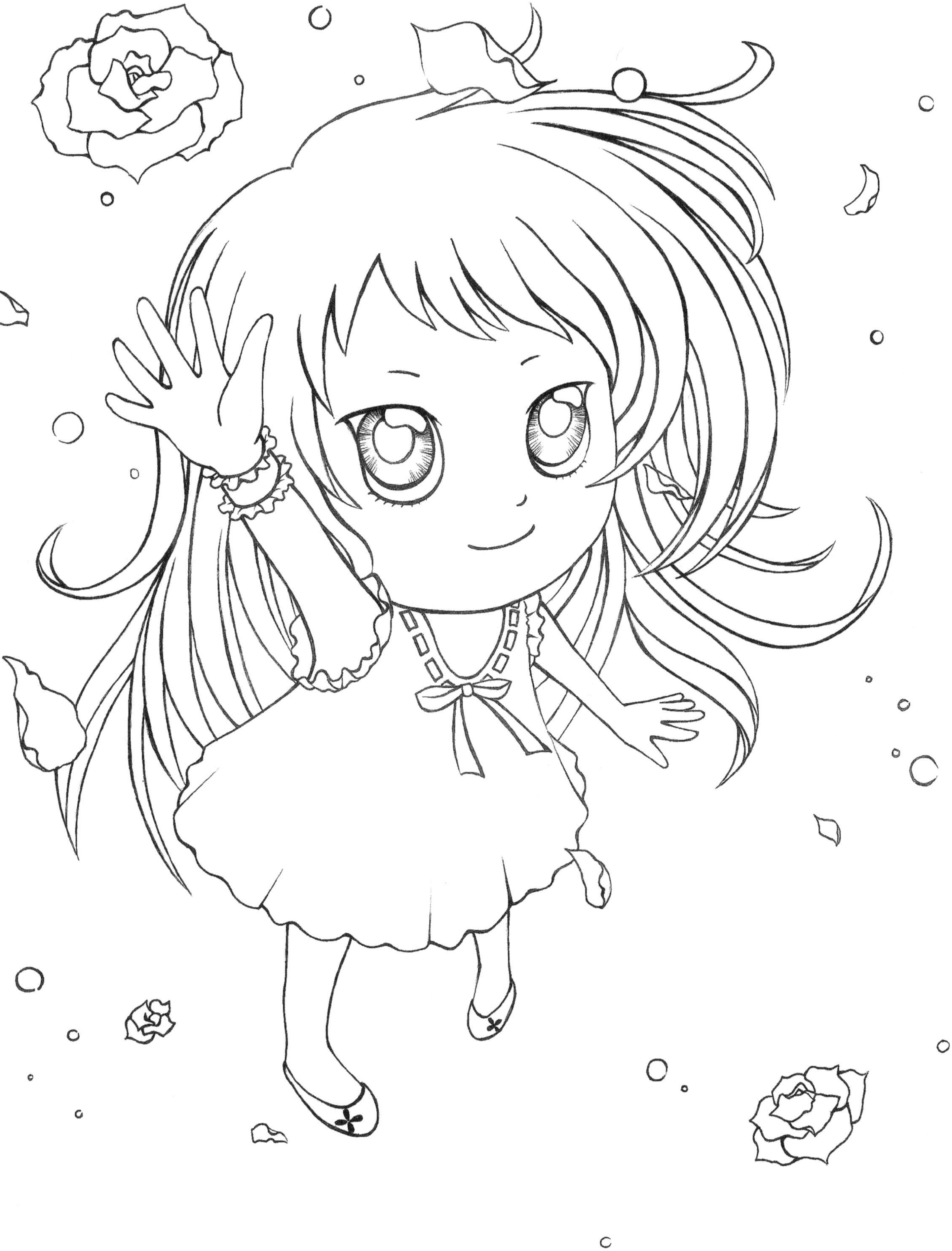

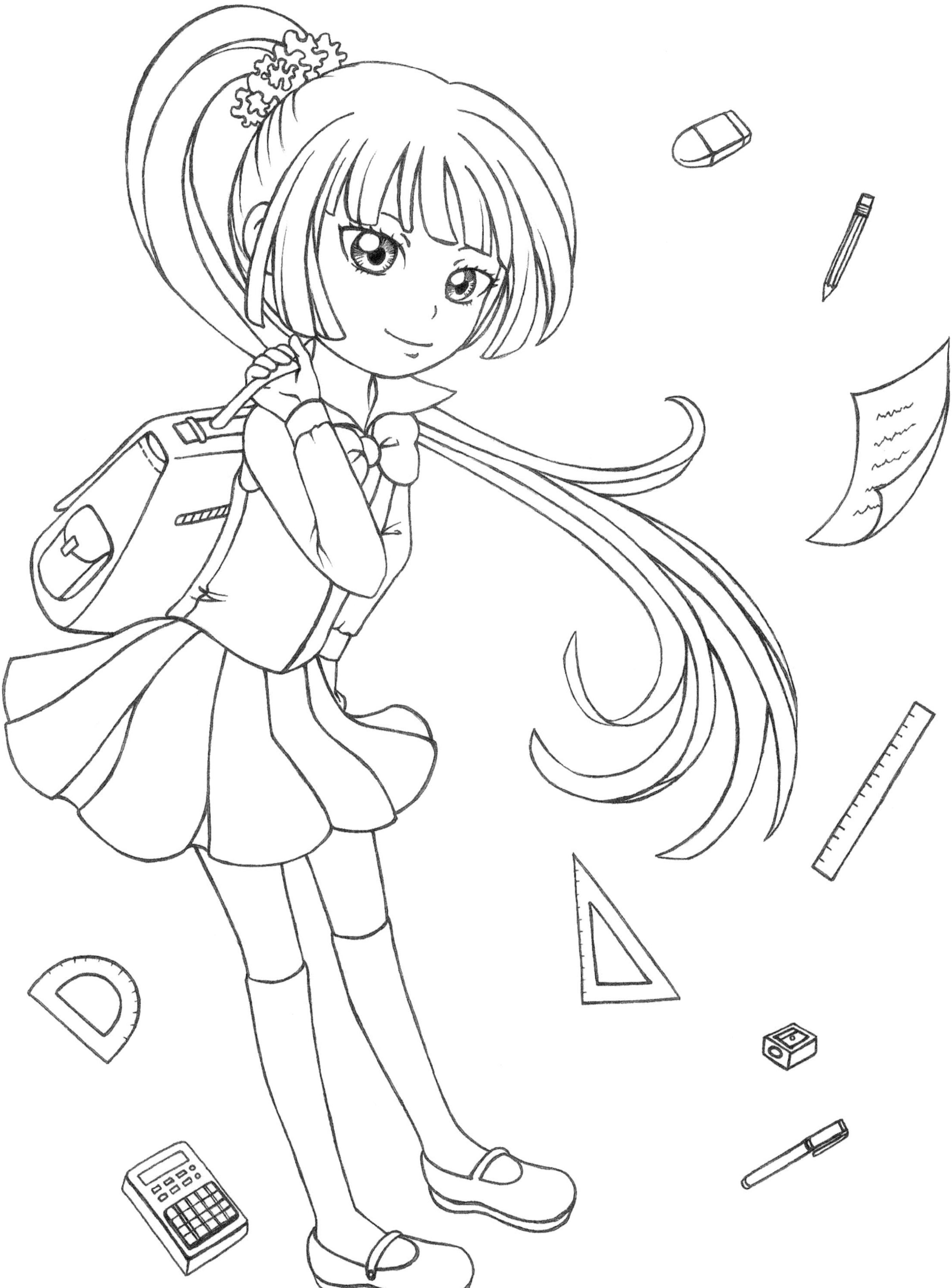

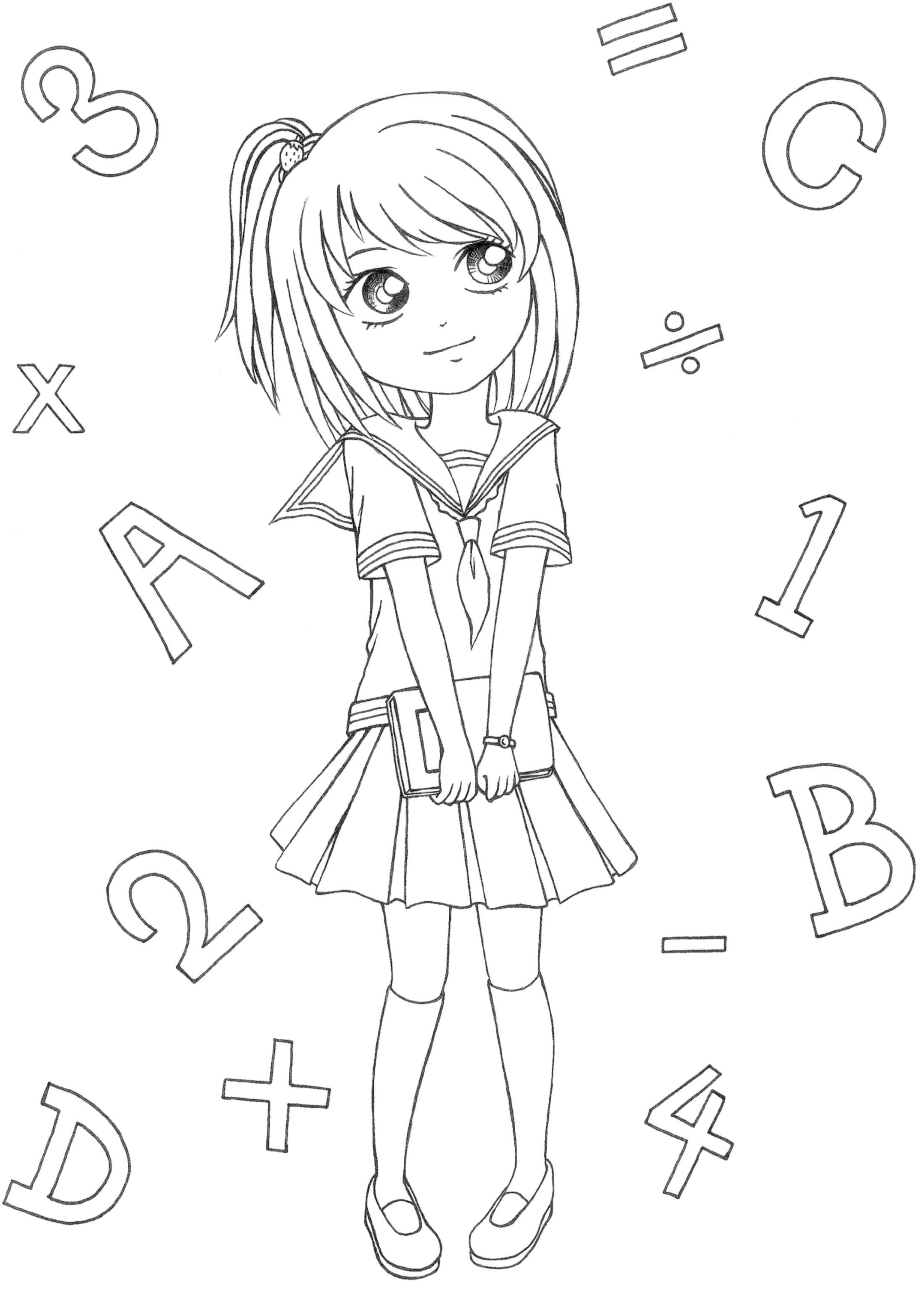
3
=
C
x
÷
A
1
B
2
−
+
D
4

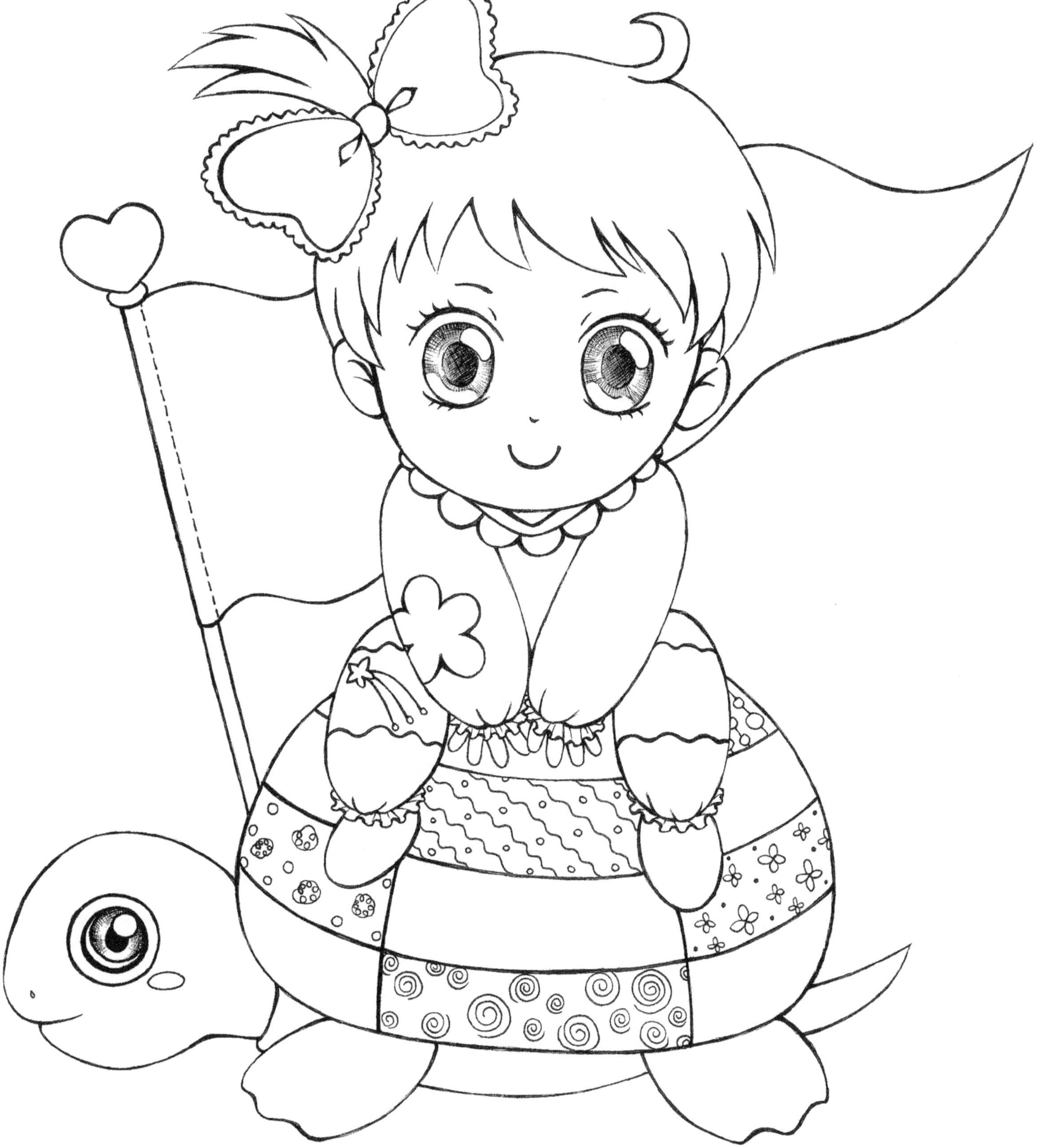

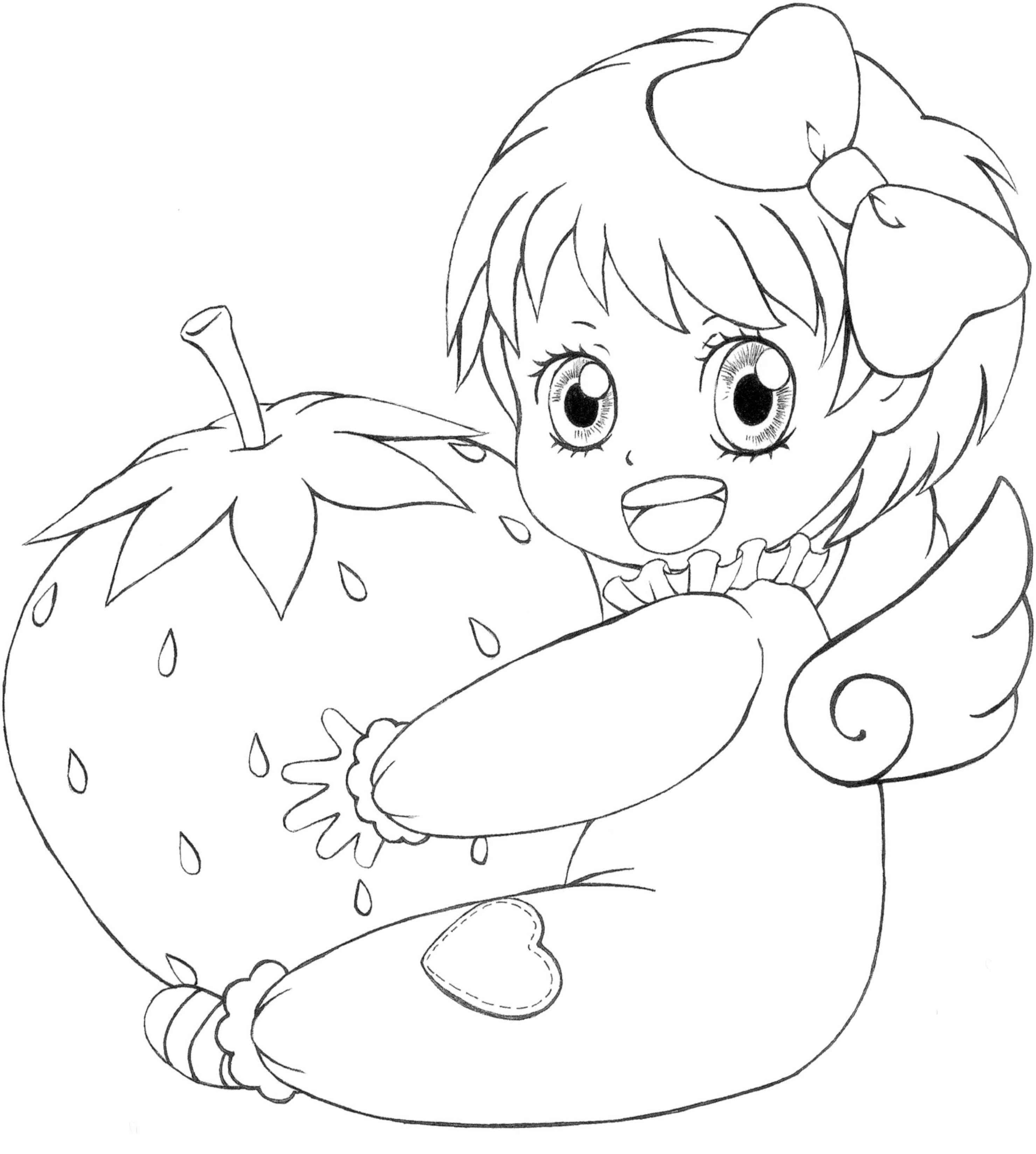

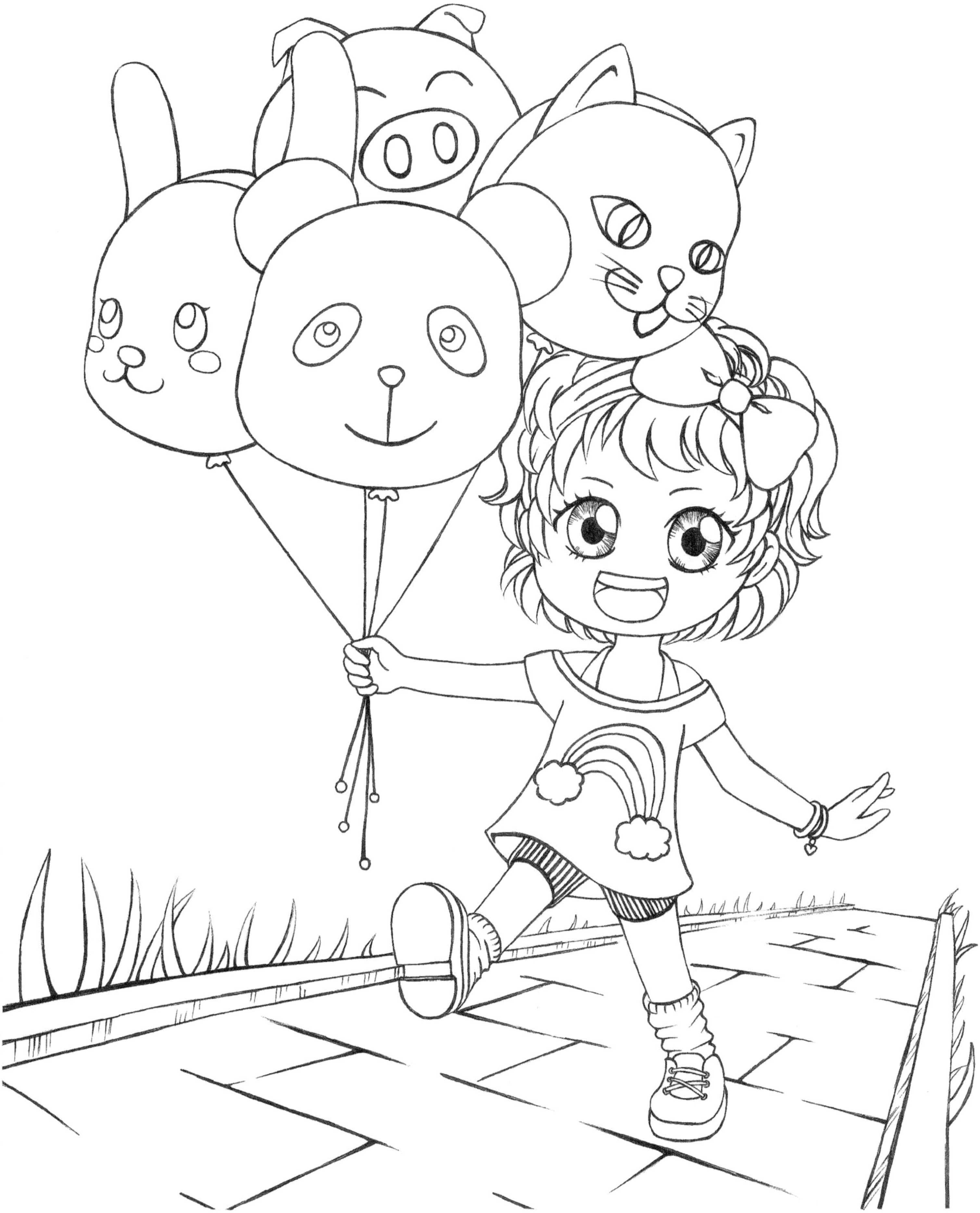

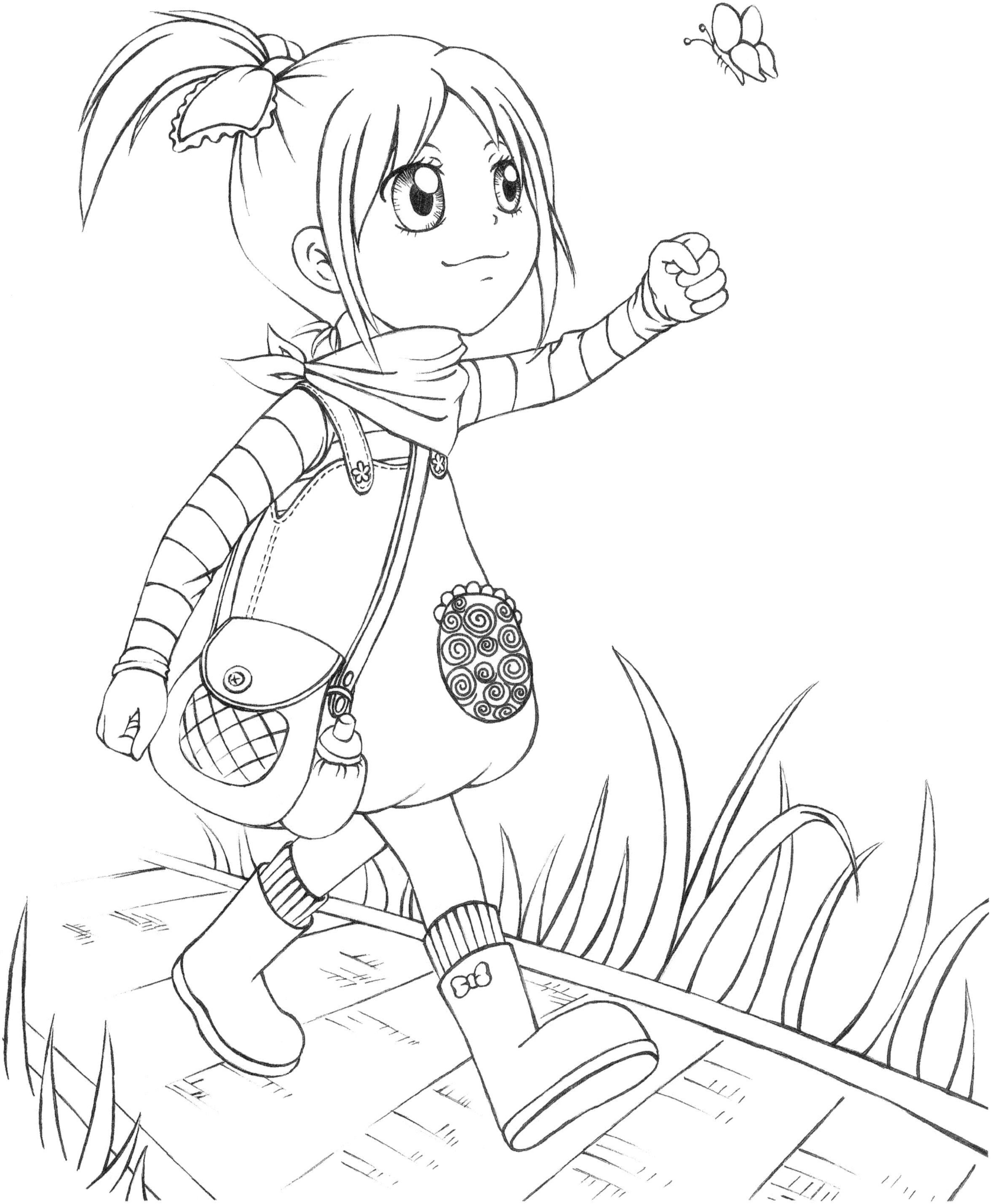

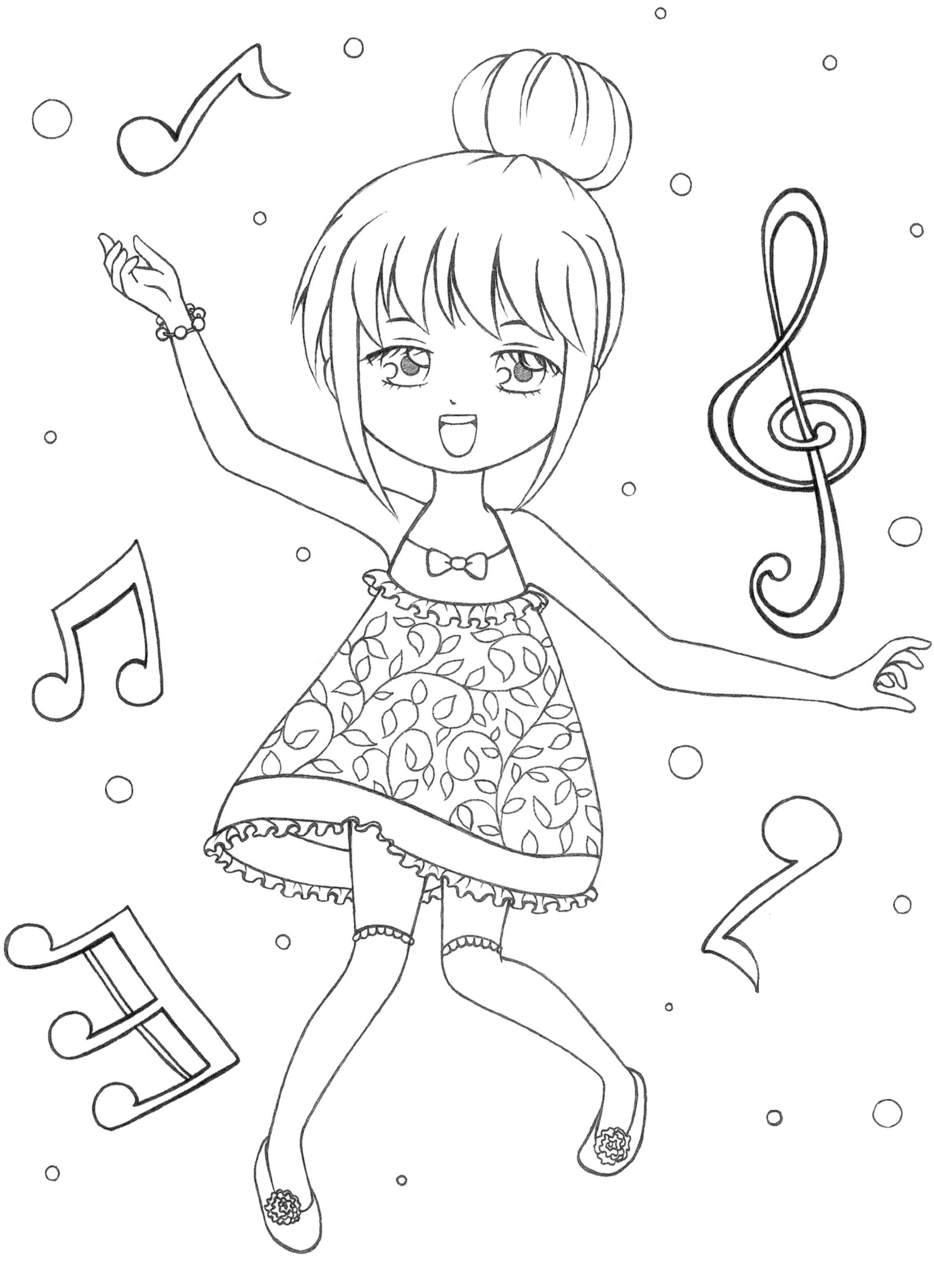

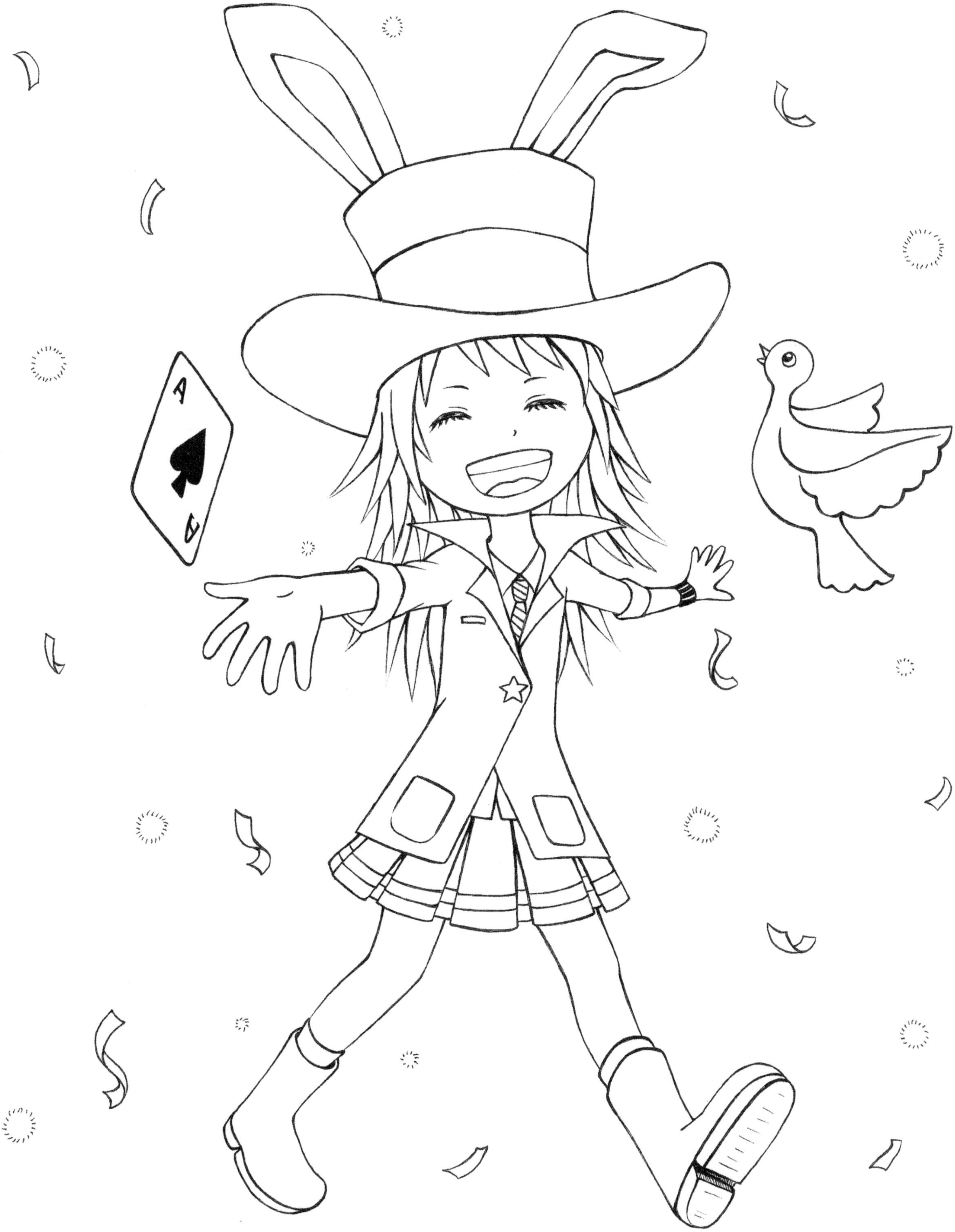
A
A

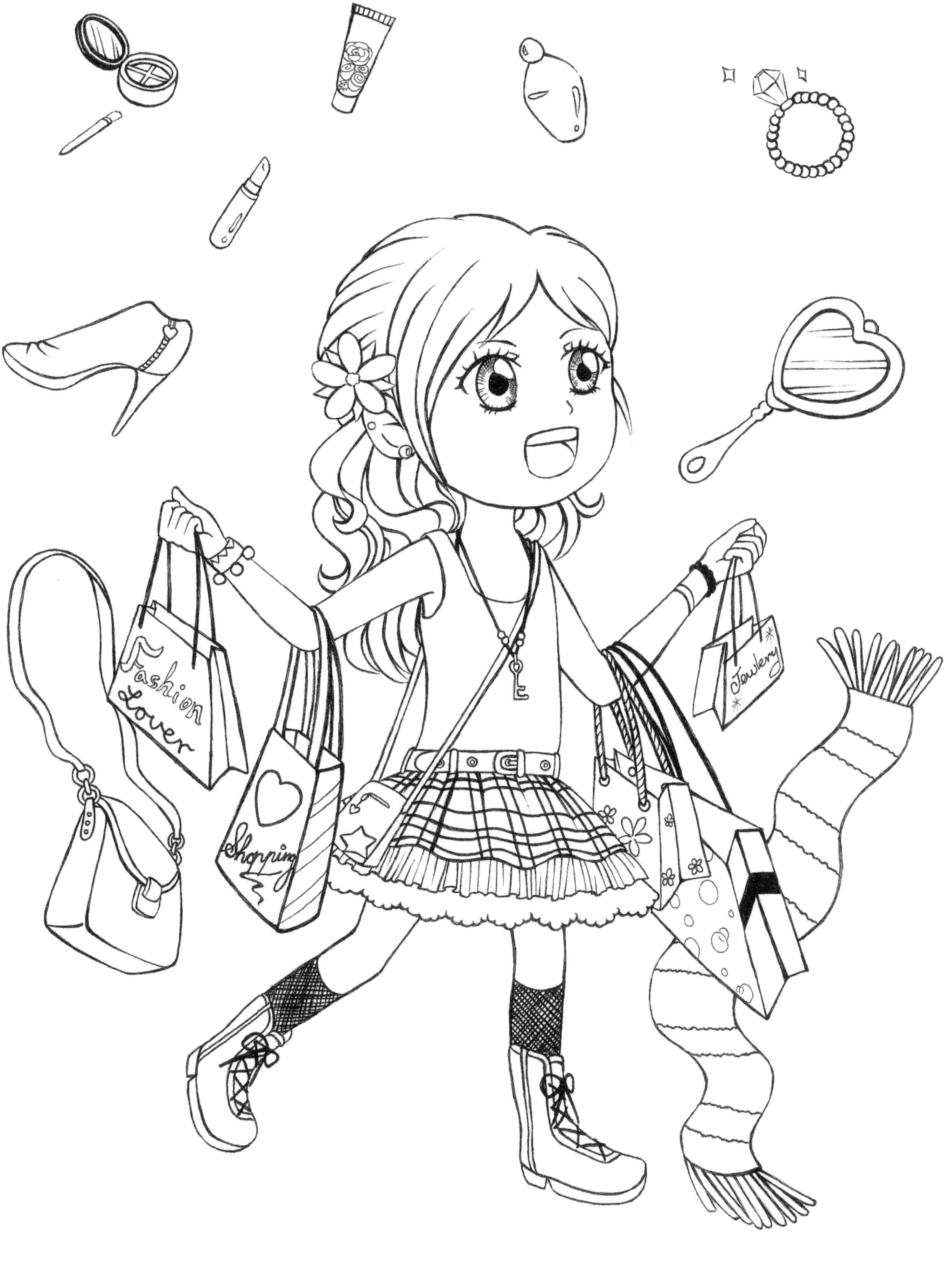
Fashion Lover
Shopping
Jewlery

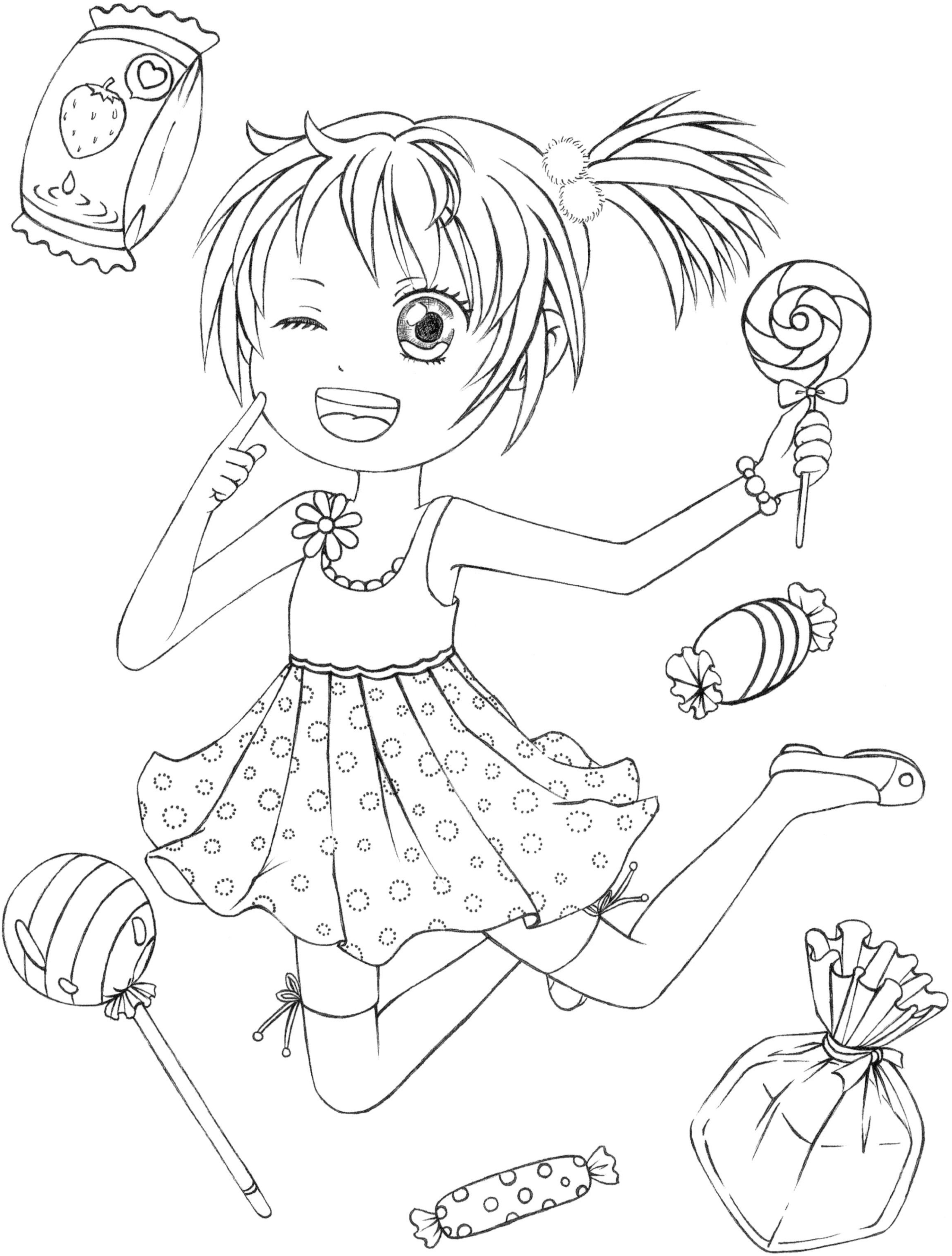

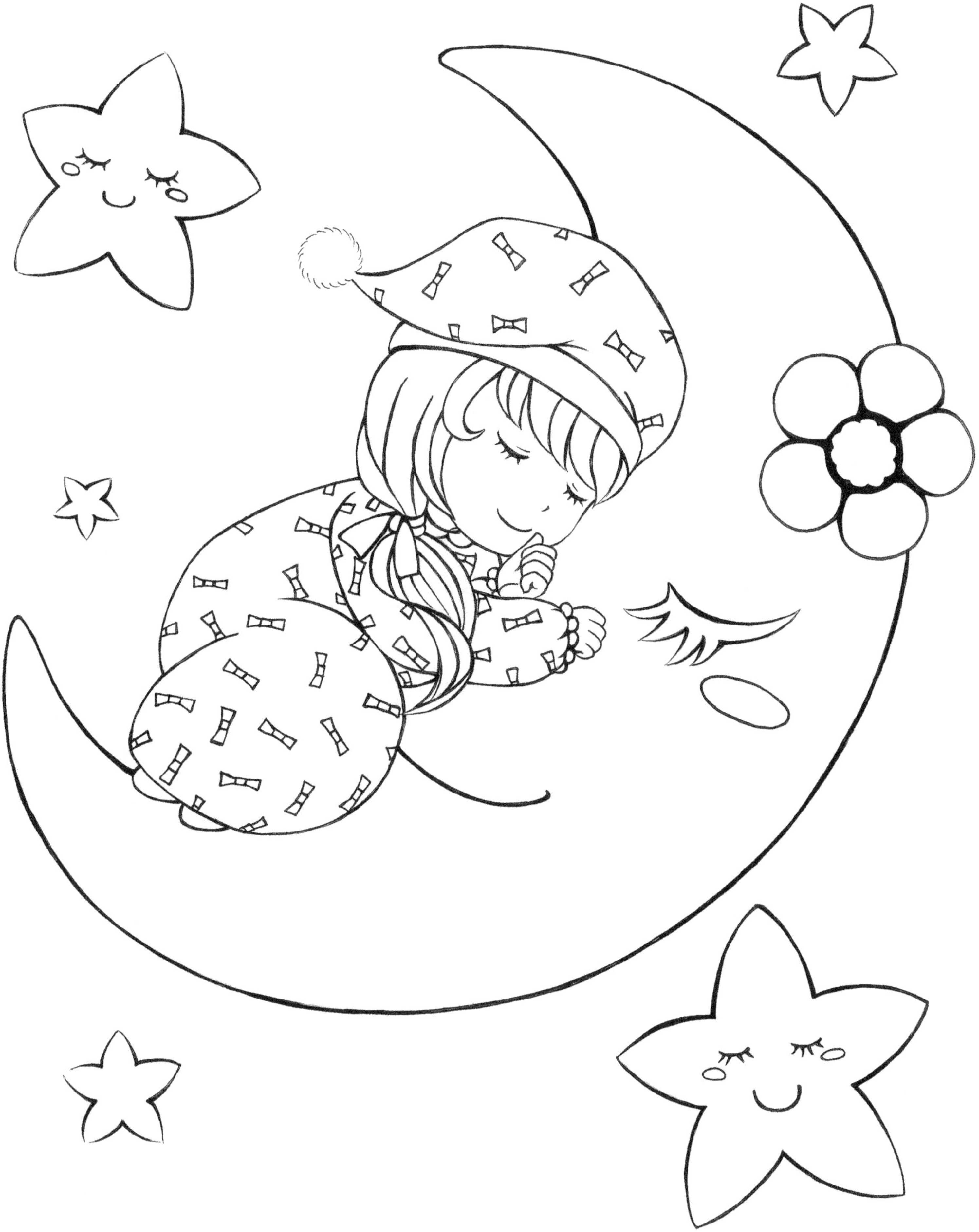

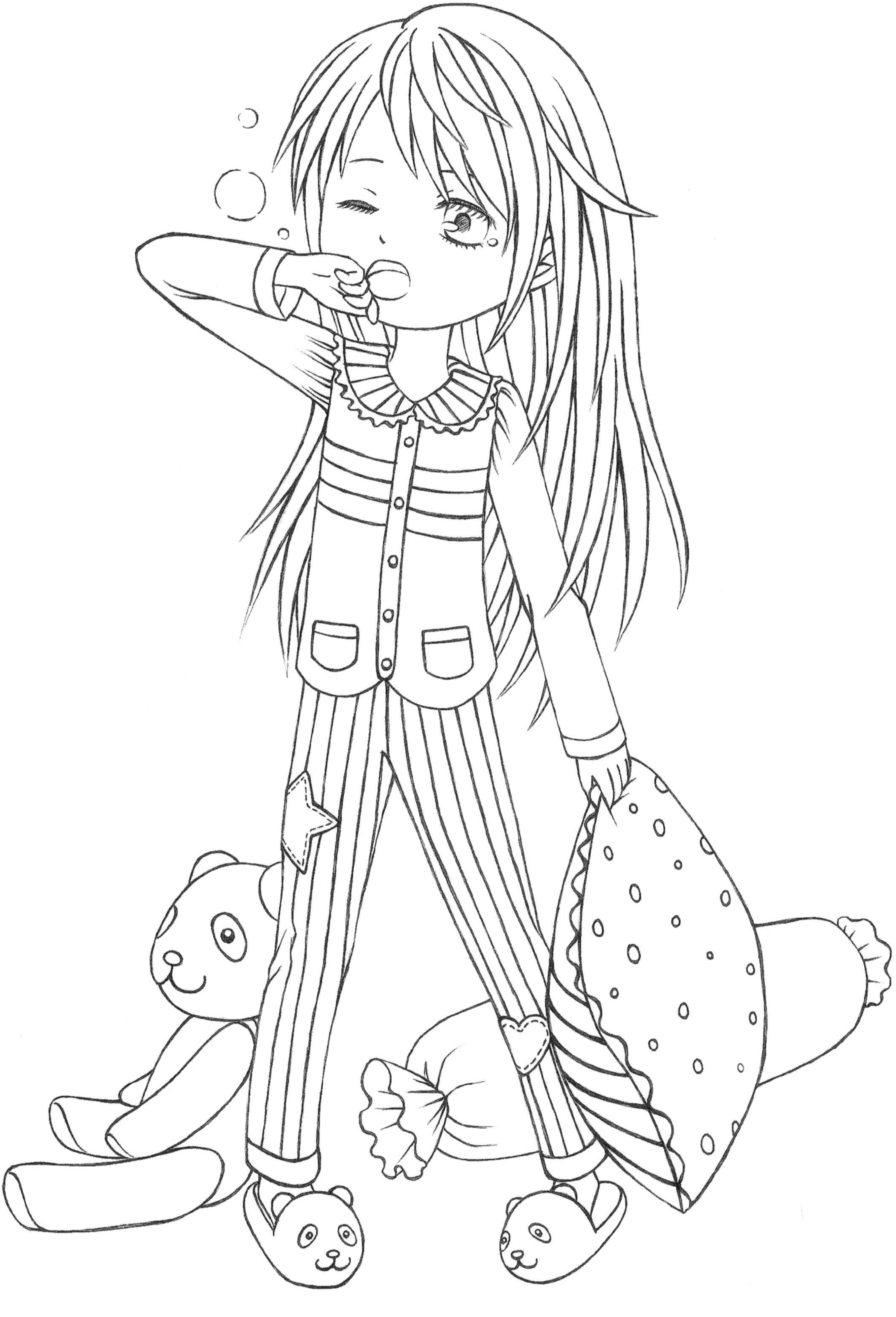

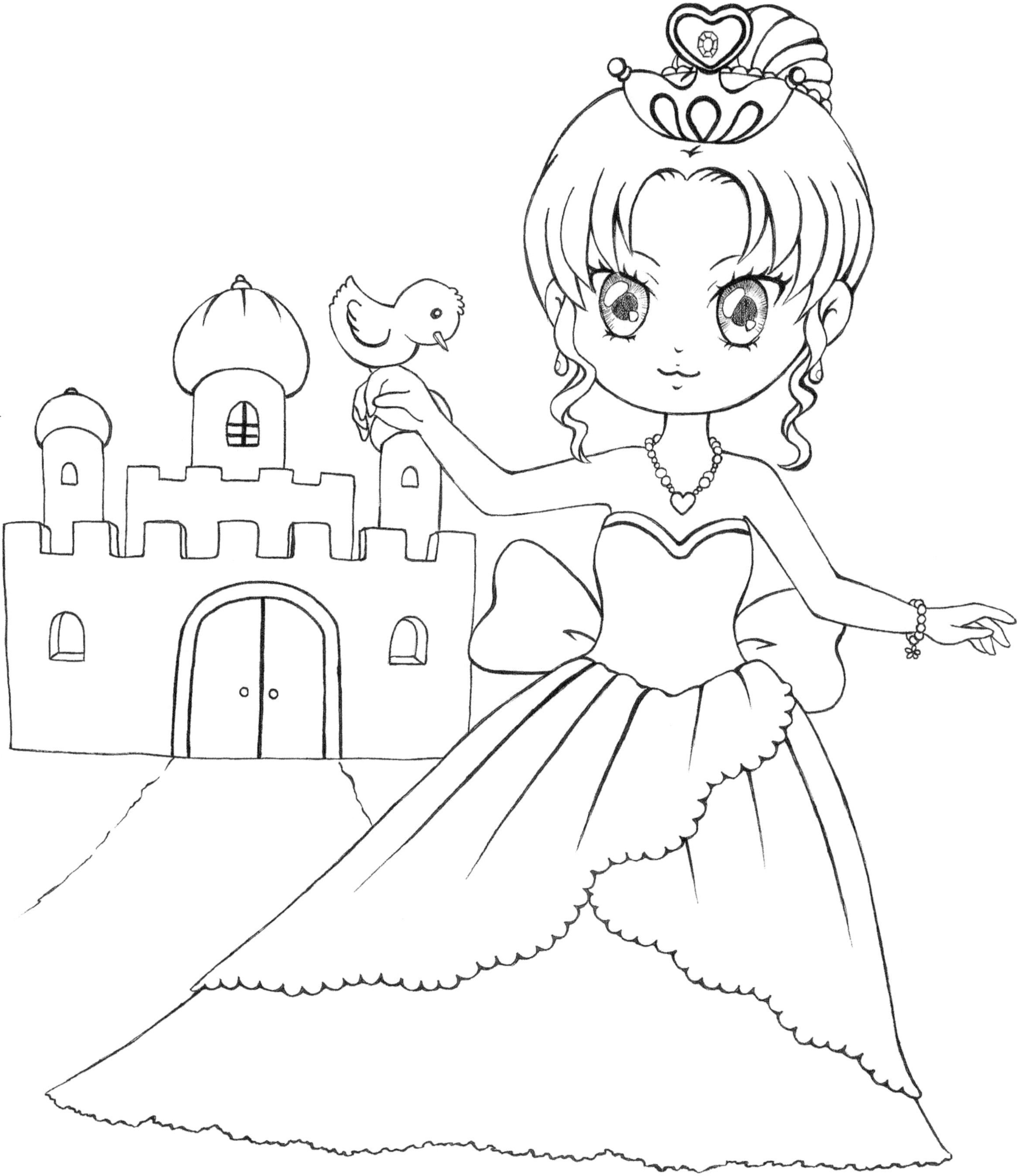

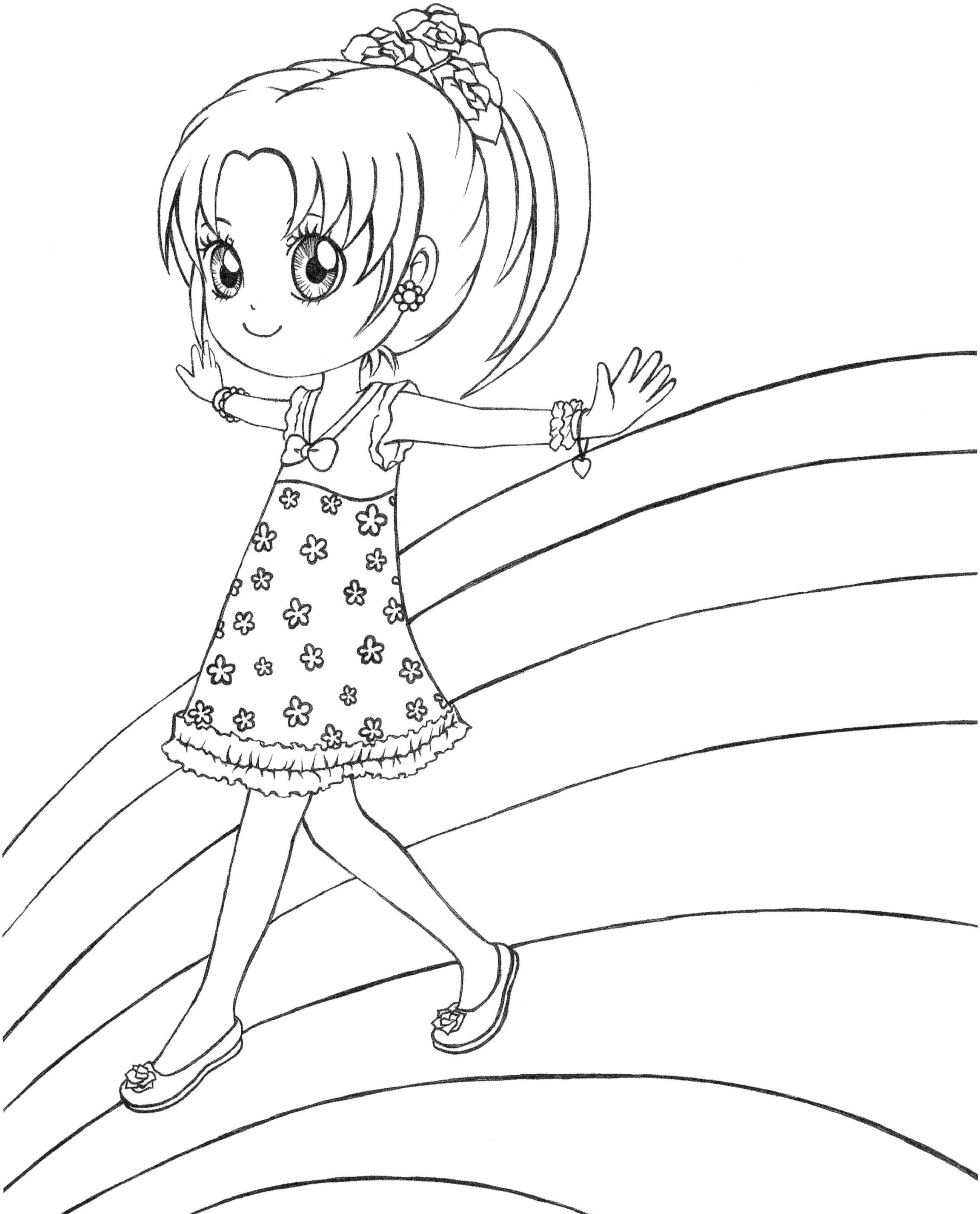

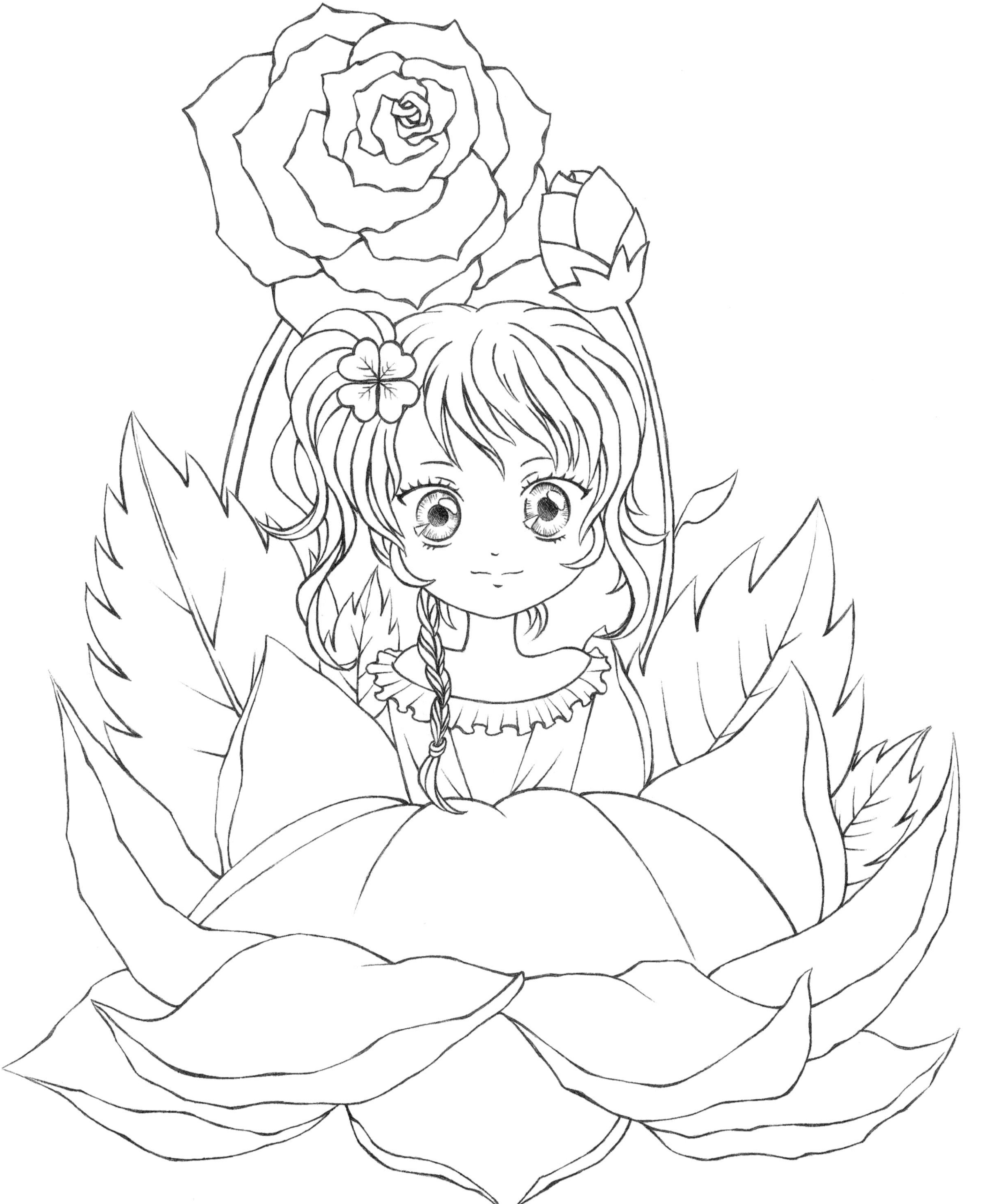

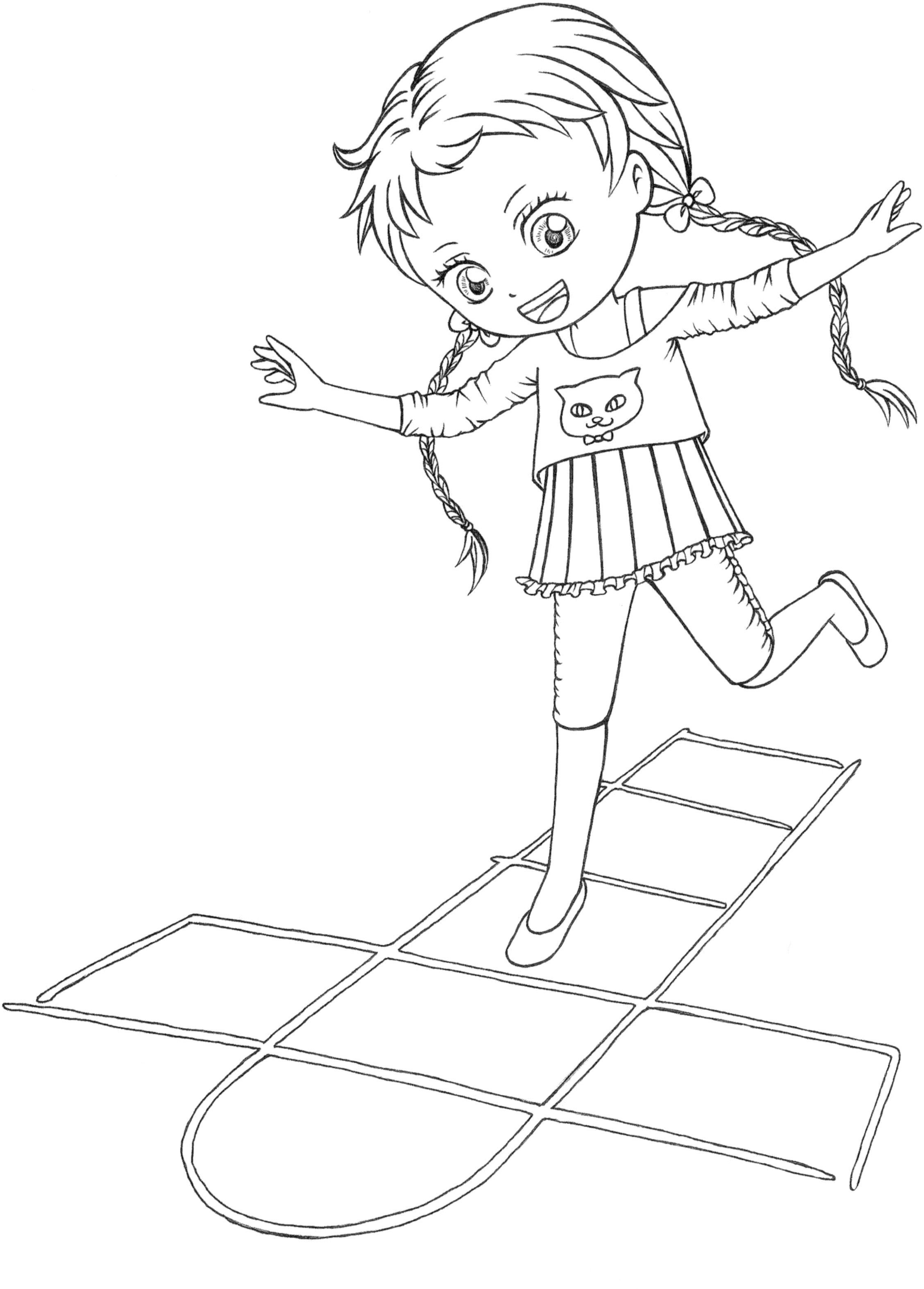

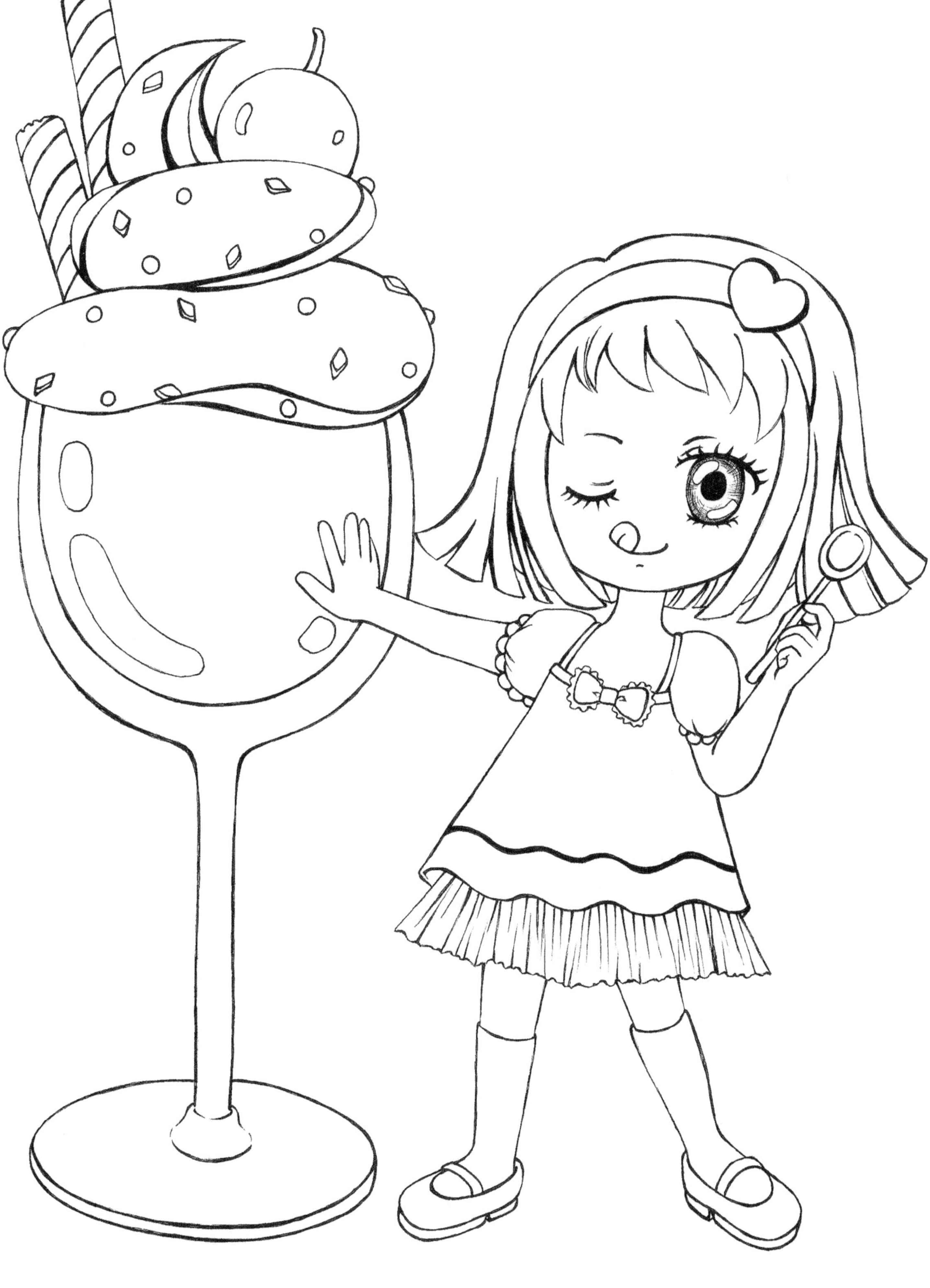

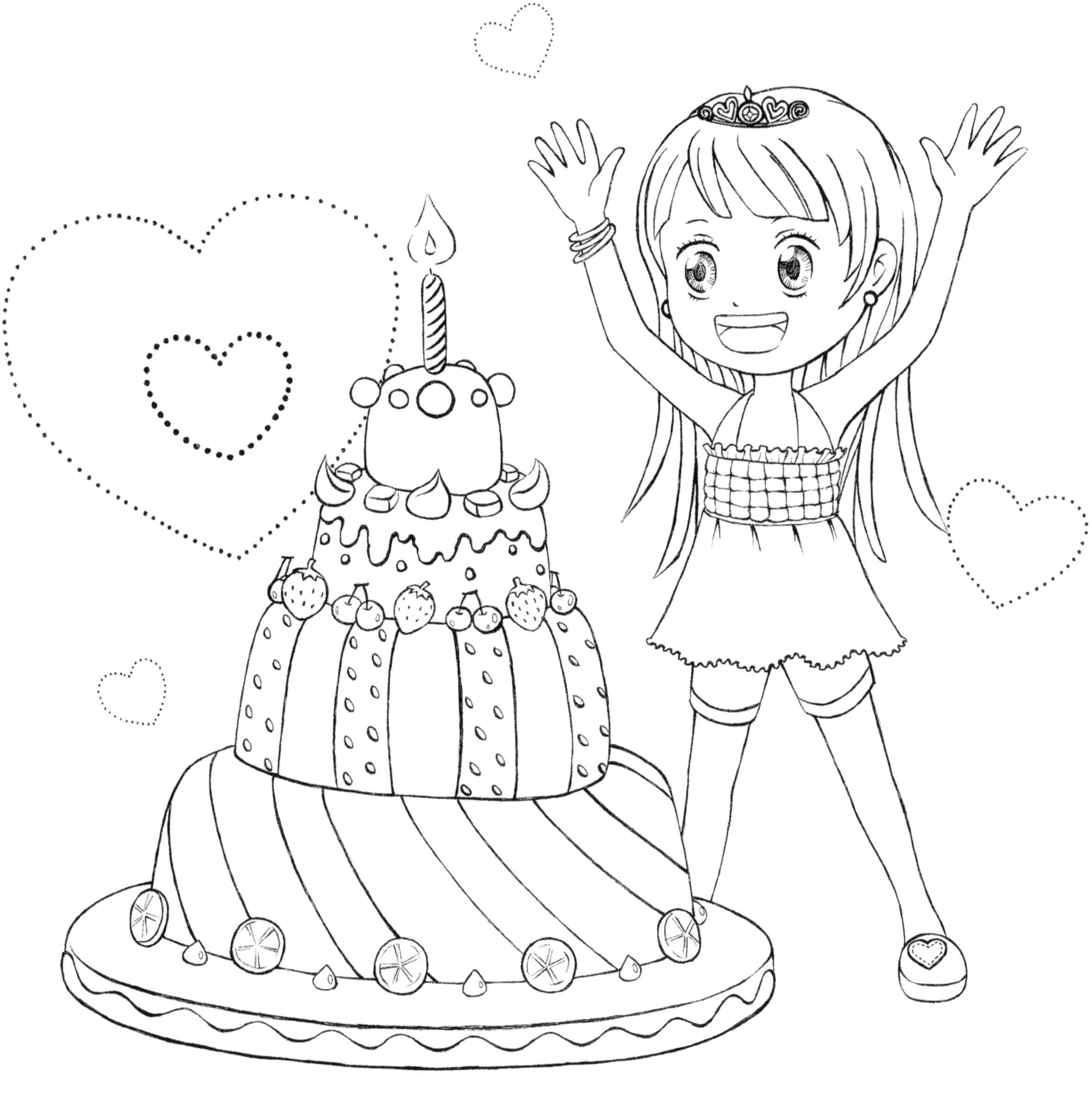

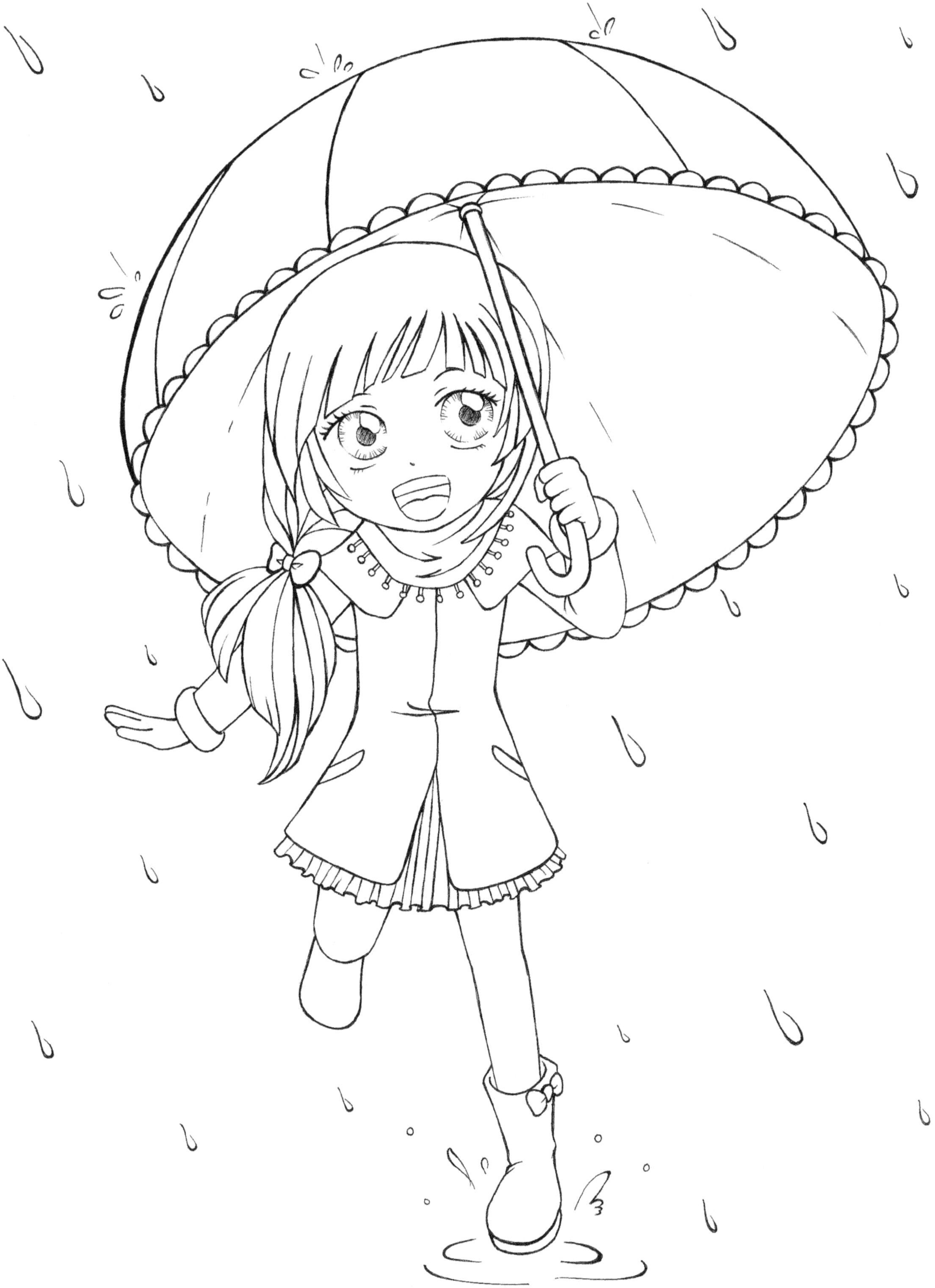

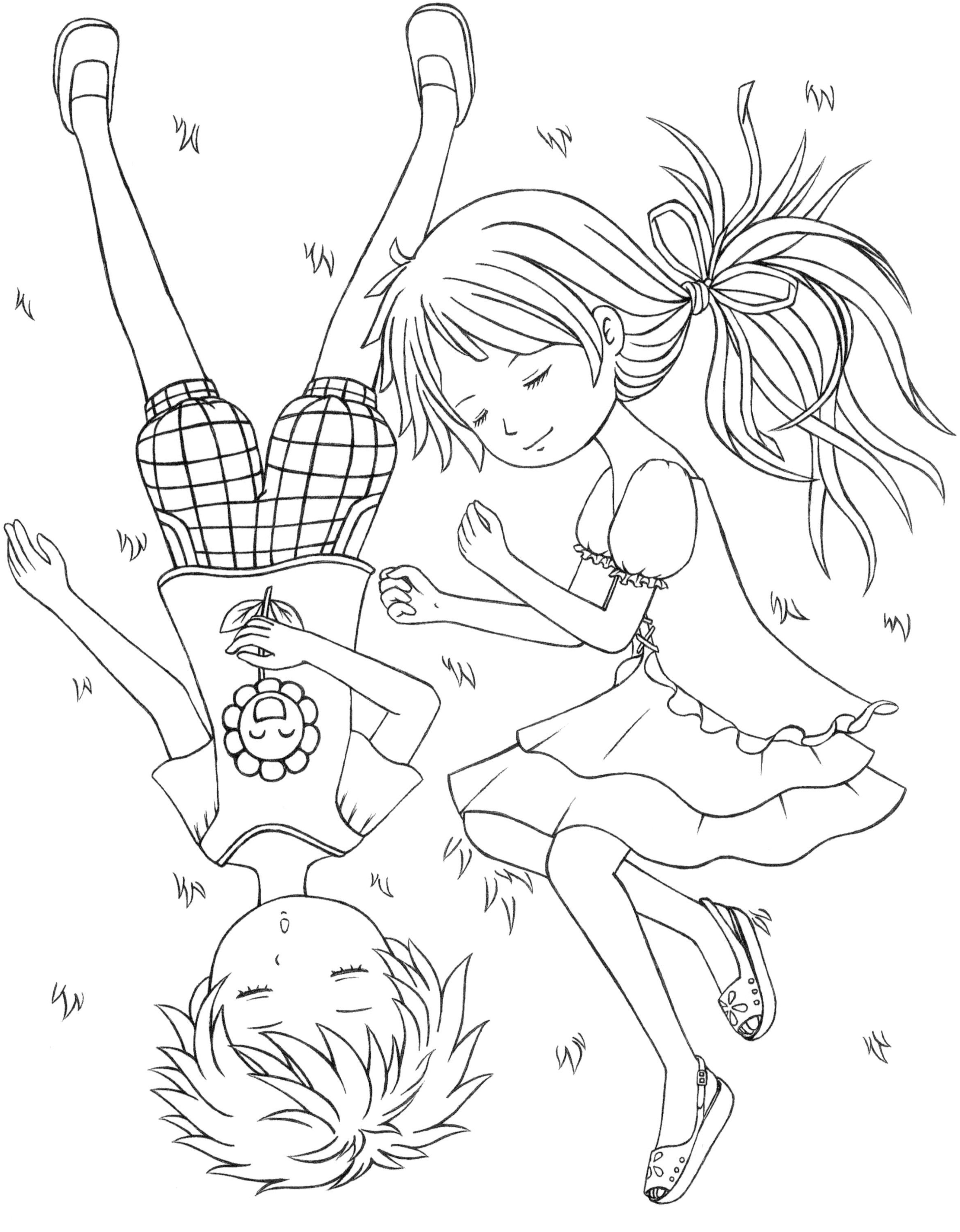

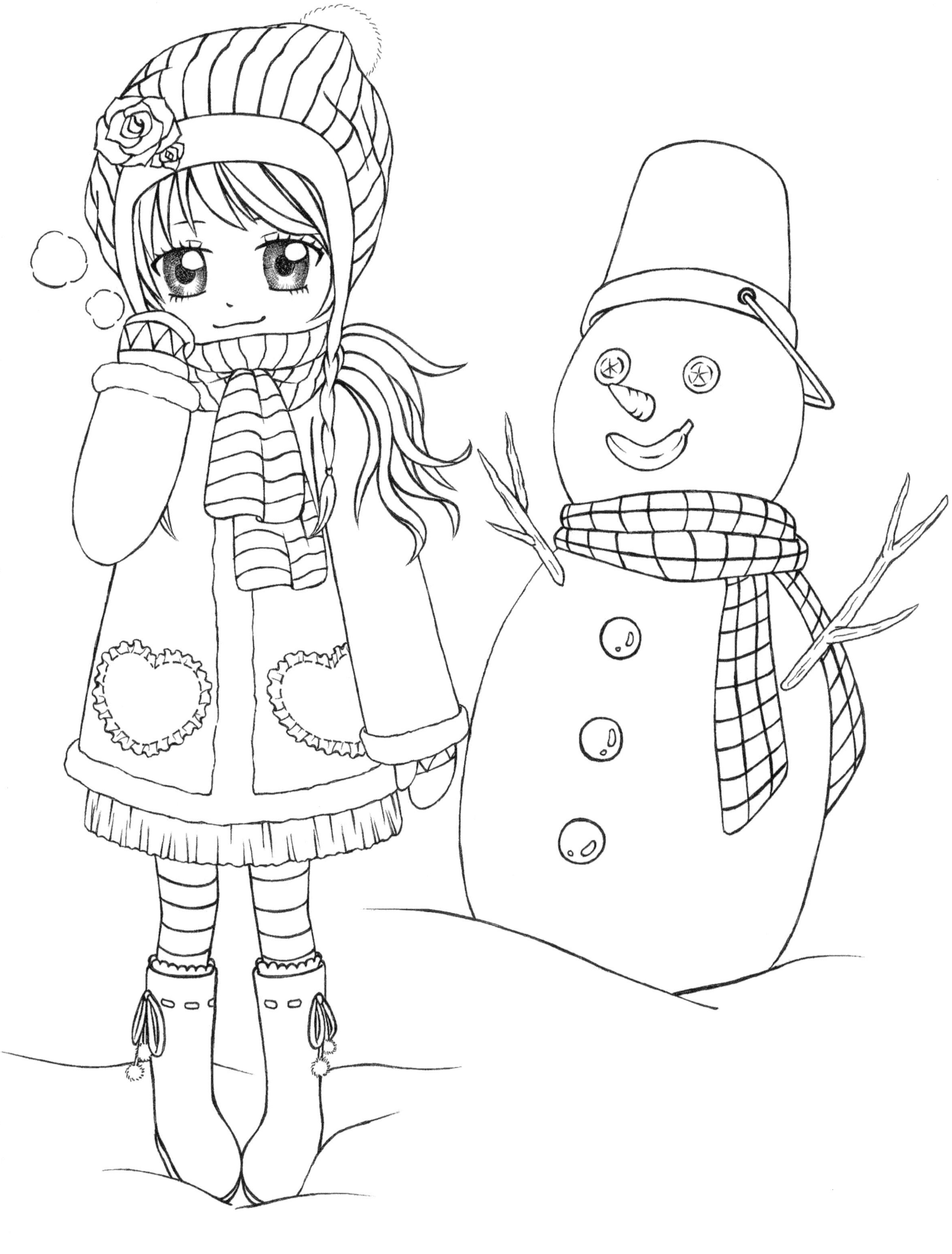

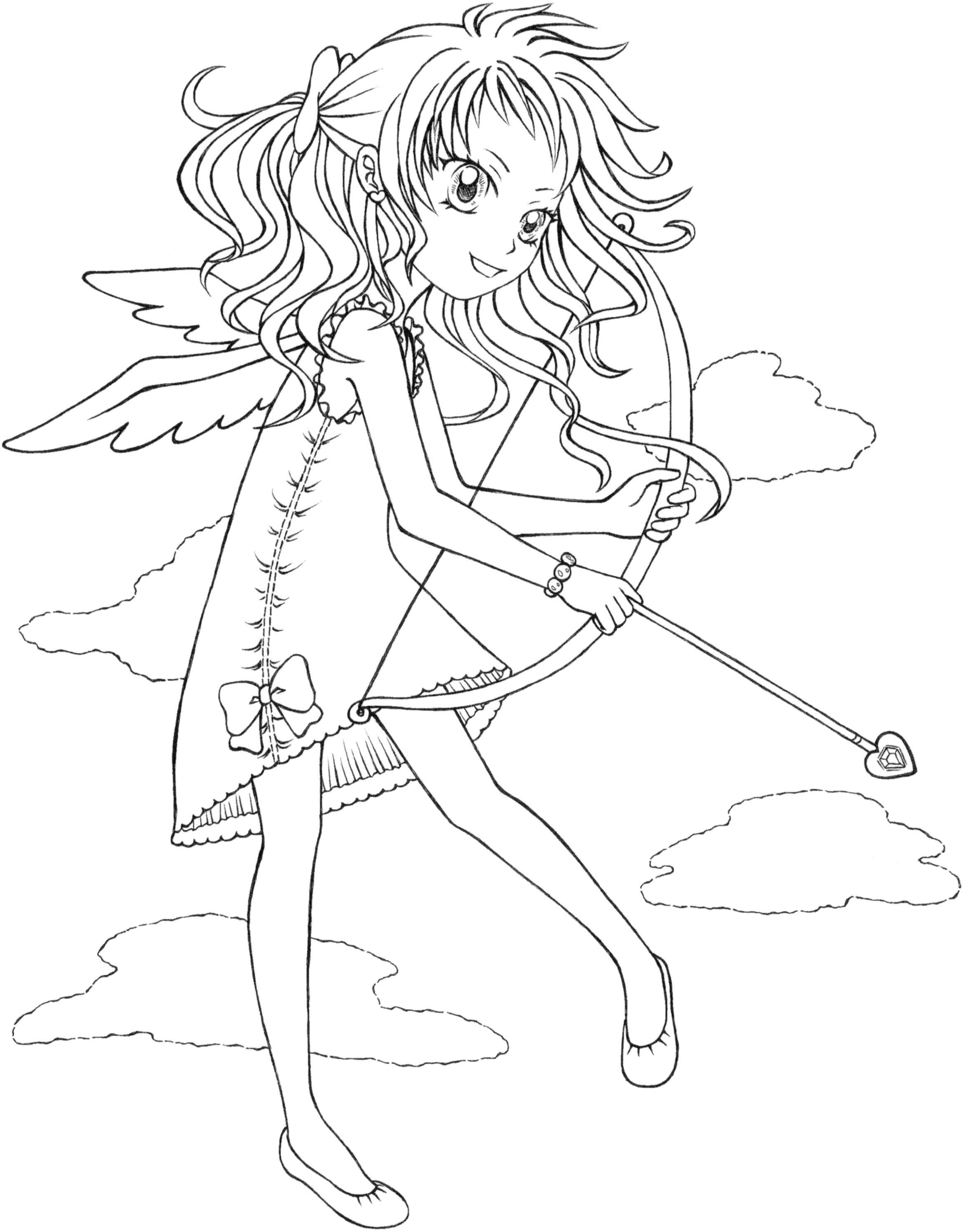

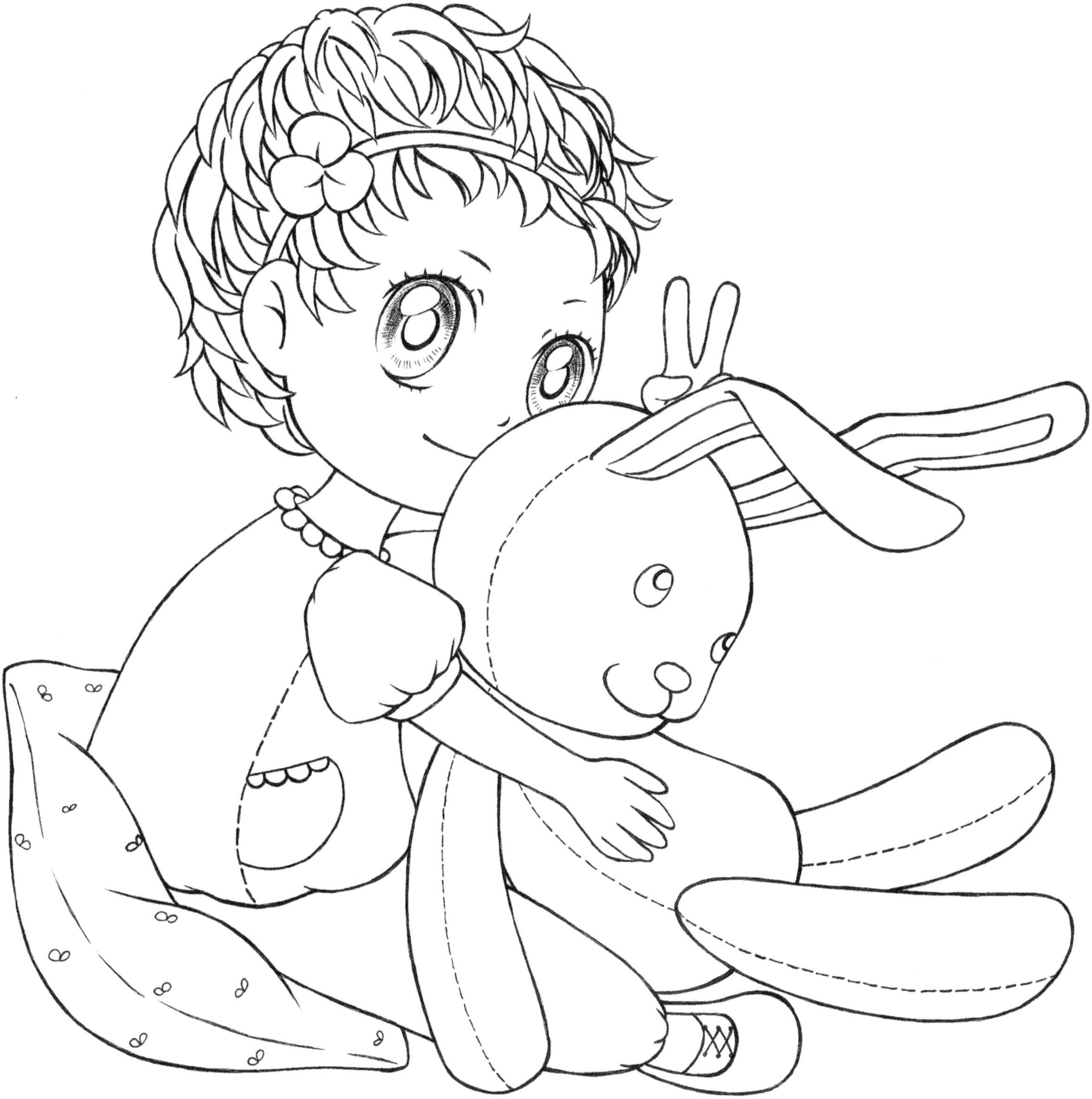

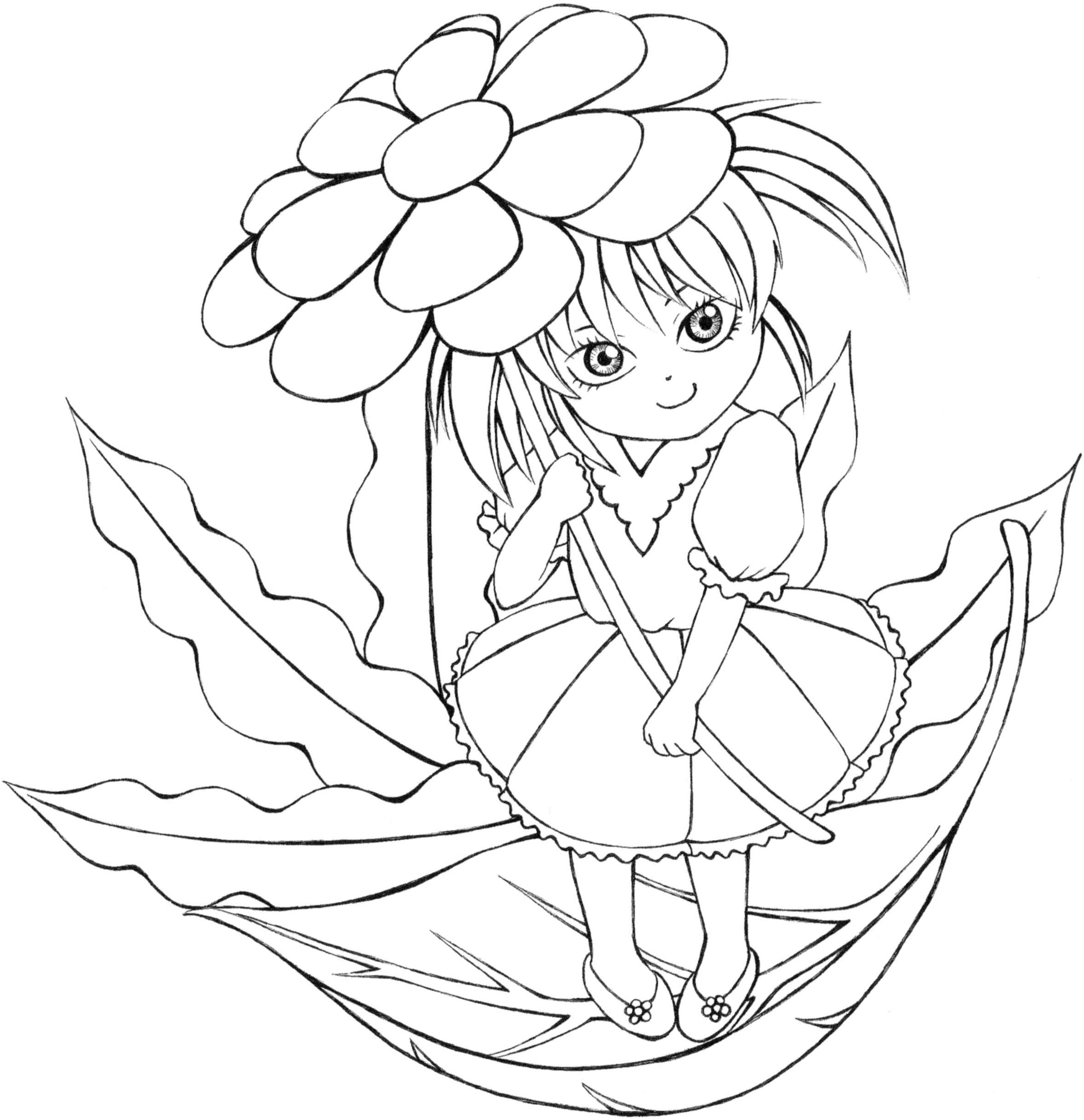

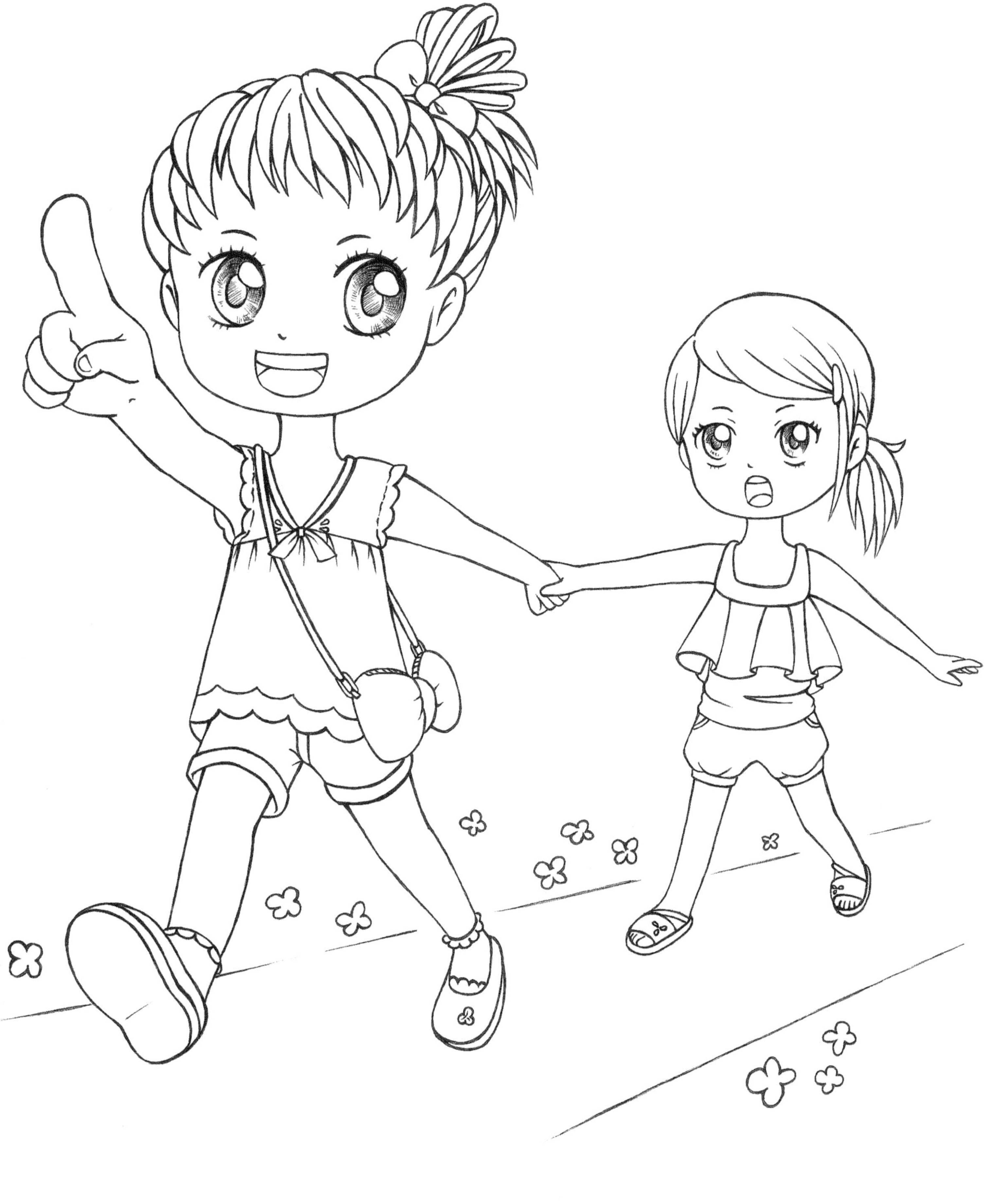

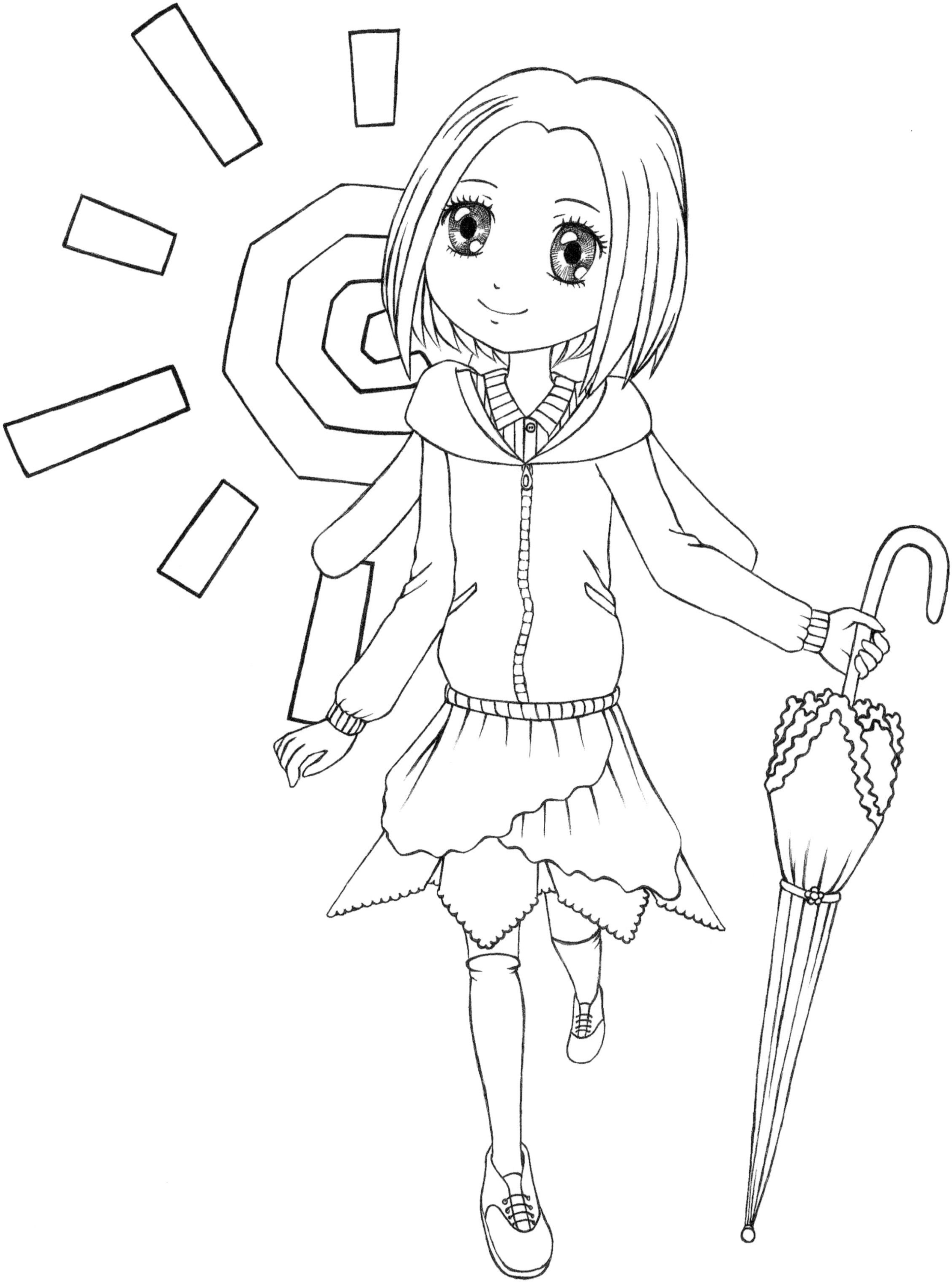

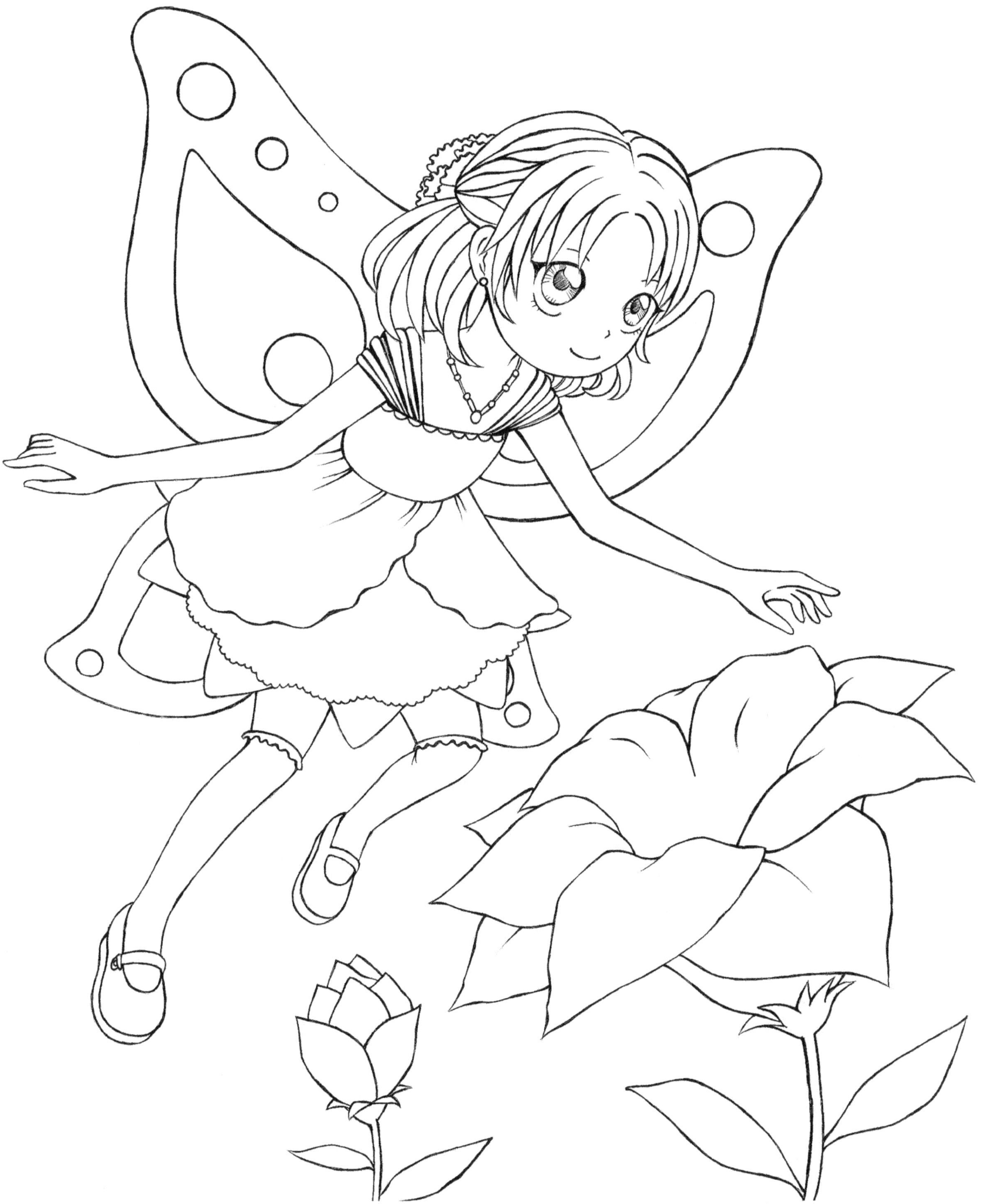

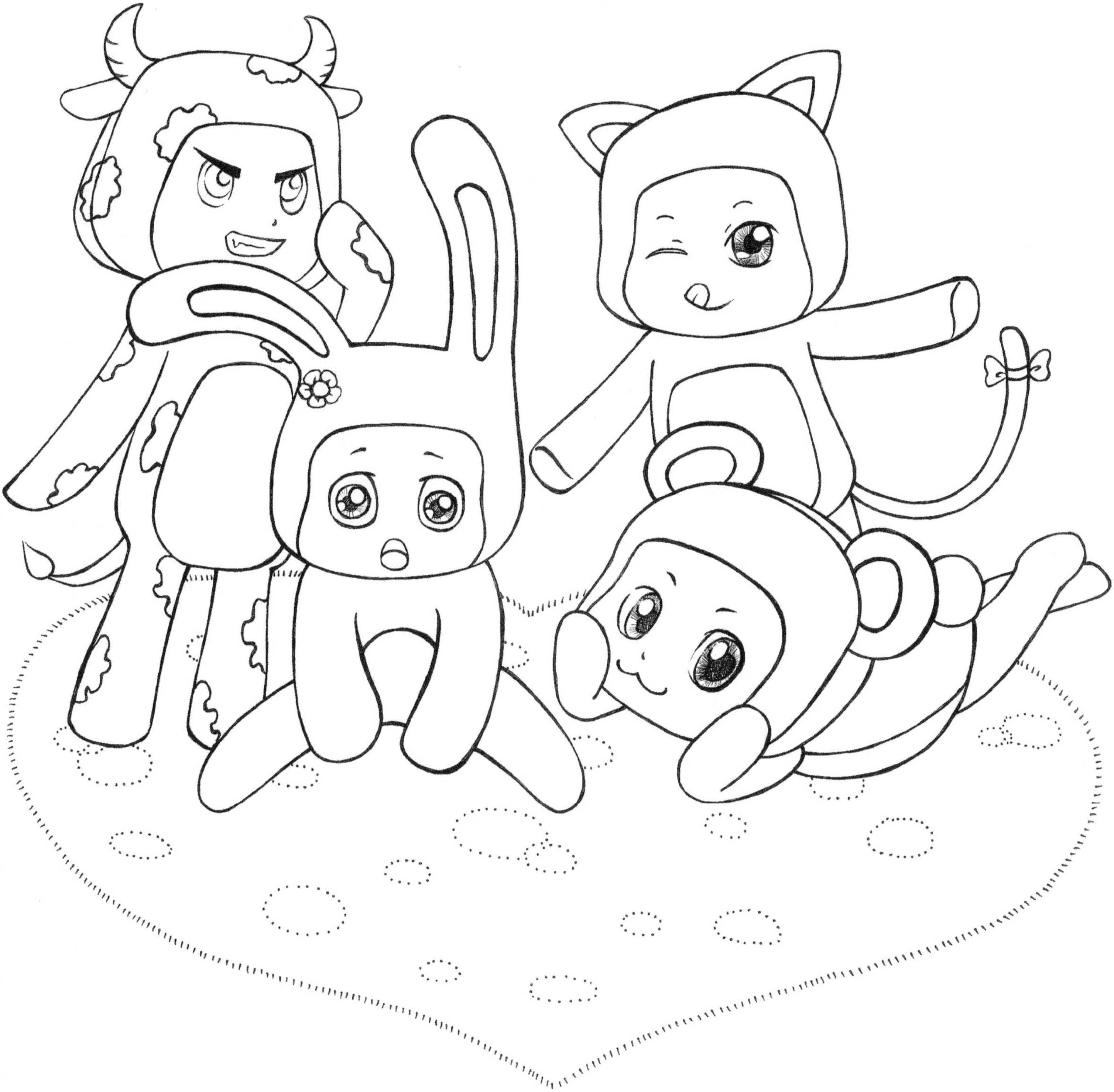

www.ingramcontent.com/pod-product-compliance
Lightning Source LLC
Chambersburg PA
CBHW080547190526
45169CB00007B/2664
9781532943614